M000074542

impactivity

what if you're working hard on all the wrong things?

TRACY HIGLEY

bestselling author and noted entrepreneur

2016, 2017 by Tracy L. Higley
All rights reserved, No portion of this book may be
reproduced, stored in a retrieval system, or transmitted in any
form or by any means—electronic, mechanical, photocopy,
recording, scanning, or other—except for brief quotations in
critical reviews or articles, without the prior written permission
of the author.

Printed in the Unites States of America

table of contents

part one: a life of impactivity

part two: the six elements of impactivity

part one

a life of impactivity

1

you and i want more

you are my hero

I think I might know a little bit about you.

The very fact that you picked up this book tells me something about who you are and who you want to become.

You want to work hard. You even enjoy working hard, being productive, getting things done. But you also wonder sometimes if *what* you are doing truly matters. Does any of it make a difference? Should you be doing more? Or perhaps something different?

Maybe you're the one the boss calls in a pinch when everyone else hasn't quite managed to get it done. The person who picks up those late-night phone calls from your friends because they know that if anyone can help at the last minute, it's you. Do you manage to find twenty-five hours in a twenty-four-hour day, to find creative solutions others don't see, to get it all done, and then pay the bills and take out the trash before calling it a day?

Perhaps you sail through most days with a smile, never seeming harried or frazzled to those around you, but still getting it all done, and with an eye on a larger goal. Or maybe some days aren't so serene and your progress is more like a lurch through your to-do list, crossing things off but unsure if the list even makes sense. Either way, you understand productivity, you enjoy it, and you're hopeful that it's all adding up to something great.

You impress me.

But I also believe that you want more than productivity. In the secret places of your heart you want to have an impact on people. You want to shine, not hide. You want to produce or create or make a difference. You want to dream and you want chase that dream.

Because of this, perhaps you don't always fit in. Maybe you've been called too pushy or overbearing. Too *much*. Or too dreamy and idealistic. Even naïve. In a world where most people are satisfied with the status quo, you want to move forward. Some people might interpret your energy, and desire to make progress as bossiness, as you trying to take charge. Or perhaps they accuse you of trying too hard or being discontent with your life.

But it's not that, is it?

Most of your peers seem content to work their daily job, come home, and crash in front of the TV or putter around the house. But you want to build something, something beyond the everyday pursuits of most. You want to create something new, perhaps even achieve something daring.

Others may see you as a bit strange, and tell you to stop working so hard, spend more time enjoying life or just hanging out, or they shake their heads at your drive. They may criticize or judge.

Not me.

You are my hero. But even superheroes have their challenges. And if you're feeling those challenges, then this book is for you.

■

If you've been pushing forward, working hard, for any length of time, chances are it's taken a toll. Perhaps your physical health is suffering. You're eating too much, or you're eating too little. You're too sedentary, or you're not getting enough rest. You're exhausted. Or maybe it's your mental and emotional health that has taken a hit. You always have too much to do and not enough time, and sometimes it feels like chaos and confusion reign in your daily life and in your home. Your relationships aren't what you'd like either, you'd have to admit. Sometimes the people in your life are resentful that you don't seem to have time for them, and you feel like you're not taking good care of those in your life or loving them well. And added to all of this, your spiritual health may suffer, too. You very much want to live in a way that pleases God and follow His will, but often you feel disconnected from Him and aren't sure about your choices.

A state of constant-busy, always running, always striving

can wreak havoc on your circumstances, but let's also look inside your heart. Do you see stress and anxiety over the scattered and unfocused way you are living? Are you pushing hard, but on the edge of burnout? Feel a lack of joy and peace in your daily life and relationships? Even though you feel guilty about those relationships, do you struggle at the same time to not resent the people who seem to stand in the way of your getting things done?

Or do you experience fear? Perhaps you are afraid that you are being selfish if you pursue a dream, especially if it involves money or "worldly" success. You're afraid others will think you arrogant to believe you can achieve something amazing. You're torn between trying to be content with the way things are and the terrible fear that things will always be the same.

Under all the confusion and questioning, there is lurking discontent, guilty shame, restless anxiety, and a nagging fear that you are busy about all the wrong things and are therefore ineffective, purposeless, and valueless.

Don't worry. You're still my hero.

■

All of this up and down, guilt and shame, confusion and anxiety, restlessness and drive may have led you to a place of questioning.

A place of wondering.

Should you be striving for more? Wanting more? Is having a dream a distraction from what you're supposed to be doing? If you're a woman, and especially if you're connected to a body of Christians within a church, then added to all of this may be a

impactivity.com

question of whether it's even legitimate for you to pursue a business or project outside of your family, or outside the volunteer work or low-paying job you've taken only to contribute to the family income.

My guess is that you've picked up this book looking for some great advice on time management and productivity. You want to get more done in less time, with some space left over for taking care of yourself. Maybe you feel like you should be more Mary, less Martha, and learn how to put away the endless to-do list so you can survive.

But God has so much more for you than mere survival.

I understand where you are coming from, only too well, because I have been there. I've been that person I described above—all of it—and my heart aches for you in the place you find yourself, wanting so much more and having no idea how you could ever fit in even a *little* more.

But not only do I hurt with you in that frustration, I also rejoice over you and your potential!

And my prayer is that this book takes you there, to that place where hope intersects with your calling, where peace overflows in your relationships and where your time multiplies in a way that could only be God-sent.

I pray that this book ups your *impactivity* in ways that you could never fathom.

Because you are amazing. You have a purpose. You are going to do great things.

productivity is killing me and i want more

It was Christmas 2008 and productivity was killing me, yet

11

I wanted more of it.

I wanted more tasks crossed off the list, more projects completed, more dreams realized.

The northeast United States where I live was gripped by an arctic chill and I was losing my mind. In the months leading up to December, my retail business was exploding and my publishing career was in full throttle. My husband and four kids needed me, my employees and customers needed me, my editor and publishing house needed me. I was working eighteen-hour days at my desk, using caffeine to keep going, and making everyone around me miserable.

And then came Christmas. I've always loved Christmas. Friends laugh and shake their heads at the ridiculously-long list of Christmas traditions I have created within my family. But that Christmas, the pressure of my desire for the perfect Martha Stewart holiday, combined with the stress of running a successful retail business during the busiest sales month of the year, plus trying to keep my publishing career moving forward, all formed a tsunami of stress that I could not withstand.

In my house, we now refer to December 2008 as "The Christmas of Which We Do Not Speak." I will spare you the ugly details. Suffice it to say, there was much weeping and some shouting and lots of pouting. And that was just me.

By January, nothing had improved. I was ready to run. Truly, ready to scrap everything and run away forever. I knew I could not sustain this pace and I saw absolutely no way out of my crushing responsibilities other than a complete abdication of them.

I did run away. But not permanently. In one of the most seemingly self-indulgent actions of my life, I booked a five-day trip to an all-inclusive resort in Cancun, Mexico, hopped a plane and fled the country.

What God did in my heart during those five days was nothing short of miraculous. You will hear more about what I learned in the pages to follow. The biggest revelation was that productivity had become an addiction for me. And like any addiction, I craved it even though it was killing me.

I started aiming for super-productivity at a young age, and kept up the pace for decades. By my mid-thirties I had a husband and four kids, I'd realized a dream of having my first novel published, and I'd built a successful online retail company. But that still wasn't enough for me.

Ten years later, I have thirteen published novels, my retail business has over a million dollars in gross sales each year, I've launched two kids into successful adulthood and have two more at home who are growing up fast. I guess I've been successful in every meaning of the word.

I have also come close to a complete breakdown.

Out of necessity borne from desperation, I've spent years devouring hundreds of time management books, articles, and blogs—searching for a way to get more done in less time, or at least to figure out how to balance it all. I've tried countless systems of goal-setting, prioritizing, and getting things done. I've used paper and gone digital. I've sworn off it all and thrown it away, then resurrected it and tried to make it work again.

And obviously, I've hit bottom. I've experienced emotional and mental burnout, chronic pain, damaged relationships, and a cold faith. What's worse, underneath all that misery was the nagging feeling that nothing I was doing even mattered anyway.

13

That my sacrifice of health in every area was a total waste and utterly meaningless.

But out of the ruins, I've also found hope.

Redemption, even.

A place where productivity is impactful and my heart is hopeful.

A place of Impactivity.

there is hope

In the pages to follow, I am going to share with you both the truths and the systems I've learned to not only escape the pit when I'm drowning, but also to climb the summit that I'm dreaming about. The six elements we will cover are not easy, and change won't happen overnight, but given time, they will make a huge impact. Along the way, God will be talking to you about your calendar, your house, your mind, and mostly your heart. I can tell you—from the other side—that if you will take the time to work through these principles, you will find joy where there was sadness, peace instead of confusion, balance and rest rather than feeling overwhelmed, adventure instead of exhaustion. And above all, the assurance that you are fulfilling your exact purpose in this world. These six elements will combine to produce a fruitful life, a life that is more than productive.

It's impactful.

You do not have to make these changes. You can continue to live a life of hidden discontent or perpetual exhaustion. The years will slip past and you will find yourself bogged down in work you do not love, keeping a pace you cannot sustain, with periods of crashing and numbing distraction. Perhaps you feel that this kind of life is the "suffering" you are called to, the cross you must bear, the self-denial of a godly life. I refuse to believe it. Every picture God gives us of the life that pleases Him looks abundant and fruitful, joyful and overflowing, in the midst of suffering perhaps, but not suffering that is of our own making because of our continued poor choices. And while there can be suffering amid that abundant life, the suffering we can expect as followers of Jesus is not to be self-inflicted. It has nothing to do with an out-of-control schedule or poor life choices.

This book is not "self-help" in the traditional sense—one that is all about fully realizing your potential for your own sake, for your own happiness and fulfillment. It's about pursuing the work God laid out for you before the foundation of the world, in partnership and relationship with Him, and leaving behind the (often spiritual-sounding) excuses and rationale for not taking risks.

It's about doing uncomfortable things and being obedient.

It's about refusing to believe that stress and chaos are necessary for success.

It's about embracing the fruitful and abundant life God has promised you.

Happiness and fulfillment are by-products of this life. So is rocking the world.

■

I wrote this book (and the additional resources on the Impactivity website), because every book I found on getting things done seemed to come from either the secular perspective—that business is a means to make more money, live better, and be more fulfilled and happy—or from the Christian perspective that work is about doing either "spiritual" work *or* income producing work, as if they are mutually exclusive.

On top of that, the Christian-view books written especially for women tend to focus on balancing the demands of home and family, and perhaps a job, but rarely do they focus on balancing an ambitious career with the rest of life. For years I longed for a book, especially for women, that told me how to live a kingdom-focused life within the business work I felt called to do.

This book will challenge you to get started, or take the next steps, in your own adventure. The Six Elements presented are all part of a life of Impactivity, but depending on where you are in your adventure certain elements are going to be more important than others. Use this book as a continued resource throughout your adventure, as you move from season to season.

Should you desire to do more around the concepts of Impactivity, you'll find more resources at impactivity.com. I would encourage you to check them out, especially if you are the kind of person who learns better with guided questions, specific applications and even a community of like-minded people to give you insight and accountability.

If you're anything like me, you'll probably binge-read this book (which won't take long), nod your head at some insights, pause over a few minor epiphanies, tell yourself that you really ought to implement some of this stuff, and then move back into your frantic or less-than-purposeful routine until you feel the itch again and pick up someone else's book. I get it.

But even if you speed through this book, I'd encourage you to take the time to go back through each section, letting your thoughts and heart be provoked and hearing God speak. Do some journaling, or at least take a few notes in the space provided at the end of each chapter. Start your own path toward Impactivity and record your journey, so that later you can go back and be amazed.

I think you're in the same place as I am. That old life isn't enough anymore—the long lists of crossed-off tasks and falling into bed exhausted and wondering if any of it matters.

No, I want more.

More than mere productivity—I want purpose, joy, peace, and life that is thriving. I want to change my world.

Once upon a time, productivity was killing me. Now I want More.

I want *Impactivity*.

How about you?

2
after hours

Melanie pulled into the little shopping center at a few minutes after five o'clock and parked in front of the Java Bean Cafe. The sign on the door was still flipped to "OPEN" but Melanie knew the cafe would likely be empty by this time. She and Julia, the cafe owner, would have the place to themselves. Melanie lowered her visor, ran four fingers through her hair, straightened the chunky beaded necklace that had slid askew during her hectic day, then snapped the visor shut and headed for the shop.

A bell above the door jingled at her entrance into the warm and cozy atmosphere. The scents of coffee, cinnamon, and chocolate hit her in a wave. She was hungry.

"I'm sorry, we're closing!" Julia's voice filtered out from the unseen kitchen behind the counters.

"Just me, Julia."

"Oh. Hi, Melanie. Be right out."

Right out probably meant a few minutes, knowing Julia. Melanie had known Julia only slightly for a couple of years, after meeting at a church picnic, but the younger woman never stopped moving, never stopped working. She had built this cafe from nothing, and from the looks of the place, it was doing well.

"Take your time." Melanie slid into one of the painted black chairs that hugged each of the ten or fifteen polished black tables in the shop. Julia told her once how she'd scoured yard sales for months to collect all the cute tables and chairs, then finished them all in matching glossy black. The warm wood floors set them off perfectly, and the tables were surrounded by glass cases filled with cheese pastries, cinnamon crumb cakes, and a host of other deliciousness. A gas fireplace flanked by stone burned cheerfully along one wall and amber pendant lights glowed softly. Melanie breathed out the tension of the day, already glad she'd come despite her hectic schedule. She closed her eyes and relaxed into the soft jazz playing from somewhere overhead.

Why *had* she come?

When Julia suggested they get together, Melanie wasn't sure of the reason. Julia was in her mid-thirties, probably at least a decade younger than Melanie. She had a couple of young children, while Melanie's were in high school and college. The two women didn't seem to have much in common. Maybe she was looking for some kind of mentor.

Melanie laughed to herself. If mentoring was the reason, Julia had chosen poorly. Melanie was far from having her act together. In fact, maybe she should be asking Julia for advice!

A loud clatter of dishes was followed by the emergence of Julia's tall and lean figure from the kitchen. "OK, here I am. Let's hope I haven't forgotten something important." She crossed the room and perched on the edge of the chair across from Melanie. "If you hear the fire alarm, run."

Melanie grinned. "Got it."

Julia drummed the fingers of one hand on the table while running her other hand through her short-cropped dark hair. "What can I get for you? Do you want me to make you a chicken wrap—"

Melanie held up a hand. "No more work for you! Just give me something already made. And I'll help myself to that coffee, if there's anything left."

Julia waved a hand toward the decorative coffee urns and jumped back to her feet. "Go for it. There's nothing like stale coffee."

The hazelnut coffee was perfect, as Melanie knew it would be. Julia brought them both yellow crockery plates of quiche, equally wonderful. The two women ate in comfortable silence for a few minutes.

"So," Melanie finally said, "business is good?"

Julia shrugged. "It's growing. But so slowly. I know I should be doing more marketing or advertising or something, but who has the time for that?"

"Are you thinking of hiring more help?"

Julia shook her head. "I don't see how I can afford to. We put everything into opening this place, and I can't operate at a loss, even for a month or two. Jeff believes in me, but even he has his limits."

"Speaking of Jeff, I'm surprised you wanted to meet at this

21

hour. Don't you need to get home to make dinner for him and the kids?"

"Ha! I've been in a kitchen all day. He can figure it out. The man knows how to make fish sticks." Julia bit her lip. "Sorry, that sounded a little angry. Jeff's great. It's just... I don't know." She put down her fork and sighed, shoulders drooping, then suddenly jumped to her feet. "Just remembered something—be right back!"

She disappeared in a blur, leaving Melanie to wonder if something truly was burning.

A moment later she was back, picking up her fork and digging into her quiche as though nothing had happened.

"Are you sure you want to do this now, Julia? You seem like you need a break."

Julia lifted her eyes, shining with unshed tears. "This *is* a break. I need this."

Melanie smiled in sympathy, but still—she wasn't sure how she could be any help to the younger woman.

"Sorry," Julia said again. "I didn't mean to fall apart on you. That's not why I wanted to meet,"

"Why did you want to meet?"

She shrugged. "I'm not sure. I just get the feeling that we have things in common. You always seem like you're busy doing amazing things, more than most women. Like me, I guess. But you seem so... put together, you know?" She laughed. "I'm not saying this right." She waved her fork vaguely at Melanie's head and body. "You know, the perfect hair, the gorgeous jewelry you always wear. You're so sophisticated and classy. Instead of a lunatic like me, scattered and unfocused, feeling like there's never enough time and feeling guilty for the

things I'm not doing. I just wanted to know how you do it all."
Julia's leg was bouncing under the table, and she took a deep
breath and seemed to try to steady herself. "It's just that most
of my friends my age," she paused and cringed. "Sorry, didn't
mean to make you sound old—"

Melanie waved it away.

"Most of my friends are happy with being at home with
their young kids, or maybe having a part-time job to
supplement their family income. But none of them seem like
they have a larger purpose, you know? Something they're
driving toward. They don't really understand how my mind
works."

"And you think I do?" Melanie laughed.

Julia made a face. "Very funny. And yes, I think you might.
I know you have your theater thing, and you're trying to
develop something there. I'm not sure exactly what, but I
thought you might understand how I feel and maybe be able to
help me figure it out."

Melanie put a hand on Julia's arm. "I'm sorry you're so
stressed and anxious. I wish I had great advice for you. But the
truth is, I feel pretty much the same way you do. I guess I just
hide it well."

Julia visibly slumped, but with a half-smile. "I can't decide
if I'm disappointed that you don't have the answer, or glad to
know someone feels the same way I do."

Melanie's phone buzzed on the table. She glanced down,
planning to ignore it, but it was Todd. "Sorry, it's my husband.
I should see what he wants."

The phone call was quick, and Todd was annoyed. One of
her Children's Theater volunteers had canceled for tomorrow.

Todd had made some thinly-veiled hints at organizational skills that could get even the sloppiest of operations in order. She disconnected with no answers for him, then started texting. She had to work all day tomorrow in the doctor's office since she was the office manager and couldn't fill in for the sick volunteer. Who else could she get?

By the time she finished texting a couple of people, Julia had moved both their coffee cups to a small table between two brown leather chairs in front of the fire, and set a plate of assorted desserts beside them.

"Sorry about that." She sank down into the chair beside Julia and sighed.

Julia's head was back against the chair with her eyes closed. She half-smiled. "This really is my happy place. When I give myself even a moment to enjoy it." She lifted her head and surveyed the cafe. "It's exactly like I pictured it, like I dreamed. But somehow my life here is nothing like I dreamed."

"I know what you mean. If I seem calm, it's only because I'm usually oblivious to the things that need doing until it's too late. I'm terrible at time management and organization. I can't keep up like you, puppet-mastering a million strings." She took a bite of a chocolate peanut butter brownie. "The truth is, I don't actually even enjoy kids."

Julia snorted a laugh. "Then why do you do the children's theater?"

"I guess I feel like if I give it up, I'll lose my connection to my purpose entirely. That my degree in theater arts will be wasted. I feel like I need it, to stay sane in the midst of a job I don't really like. But at the same time, it's keeping me so busy that I'm tired all the time and not taking care of myself." She

24

finished the brownie with a twinge of guilt.

"I hear you. I don't do anything for myself except stand on my feet all day, and with nothing but pastries around me, most of what I eat is not that great for my body, but I feel like I need the sugar to keep going."

"My husband would love it if I quit the theater. I think he resents the time I spend there and feels like I'm not pulling my weight at home. But then I resent the fact that he doesn't care if I leave the theater behind."

They sat in silence for a minute or two until Julia spoke.

"Well, this was encouraging."

Melanie laughed. "Sorry I'm more about commiserating than helping."

"How did we get here, Melanie? Exhausted and frazzled, worried that we're doing the wrong things or not doing the right things."

"I don't know. But somehow talking it out with you makes me realize that I need help. We need help. We can't keep going like this."

◼

One week later, Melanie pulled her car into the Java Bean Cafe parking lot at a little after 5:00. She was running late, and it looked like the others had already arrived.

She jingled her way through the cafe door and waved a hand at Julia, who was setting out plates of random food on one of the larger black tables. Two other women sat at the table—Wanda, whom Melanie had invited, and a young friend of Julia's whom Melanie had never met.

In the week since their mutual complaint session, she and Julia had agreed that they needed some other kindred spirits, and hopefully some who would have this whole business-and-personal-life-balance thing figured out. They each promised to recruit as many other like-minded women as they could, and meet back here at the cafe tonight.

Melanie had been able to find exactly *one*, and it looked like Julia's count was the same.

"Hey," she hurried to a chair and tossed her purse on it. "Sorry I'm late. Need any help, Julia?"

"Nope, I'm about done pawning off my leftovers on all of you." She set a bowl of pasta salad on the table. "Anything to drink?"

"I'll get some water."

She crossed to the water carafe and took in their motley assortment while filling a cup. Beside the tall and wiry Julia sat Wanda, the oldest of them in her fifties, who had run a successful restaurant in the nearby city for years. Her pale skin was heavily lined, beyond her years it seemed, and her mousy-brown hair was graying at the temples—whether left that way by choice or by default, Melanie didn't know. Hopefully she would have some great advice on business life for all of them, but especially for Julia, since she was in the same food service industry. Julia's friend, the one she had described to Melanie as "the beautiful Gabrielle" had flawless dark skin and a mass of gorgeous black hair, and looked more like a model for bridal magazines than a wedding planner. Julia had explained that she was in her twenties and worked for a florist, but apparently had big plans for a freelance wedding planning business she was in the process of creating. Melanie could practically feel the energy and vitality coming off of her.

So that was it. Only four. All their hopes were riding on Wanda, since the young Gabrielle hadn't even begun her own business yet. And it was rather pitiful to be so hopeful for Wanda's advice, since in the three years since Melanie had known Wanda, she had always found the woman to be rather negative.

Julia was already explaining their sad session the previous week when Melanie returned to the table.

"So we decided to find as many women as we could who were like us—business-minded, busy, entrepreneurial—and hopefully glean some good insight into how to make it all work."

"Sounds like a good idea." Wanda crunched into a chicken panini. "When do they get here?"

"Apparently, we're it." Melanie shrugged. "I thought about everyone I know at church, which admittedly isn't that many people since I'm too busy to get very involved, and I only came up with you, Wanda."

Julia nodded. "Same here. Gabrielle goes to church in Newport, but I met her at an event we were both working, and she told me about her business dreams." Julia's telltale nervous leg was bouncing, probably because she was thinking of so many unfinished things she should be doing in the kitchen.

Gabrielle's glance was darting from woman to woman. "I don't understand. Why is it so hard to find others?"

Melanie sighed. "You tell me, Gabrielle. How many other women your age are planning to start their own company soon?"

Gabrielle shook her head. "They're all just finishing college and looking for jobs. I went for a few semesters, but then knew I wanted to go a different direction. Most of my friends think of me as a college dropout, but when I look at them I feel like their aspirations are so small. I feel like a misfit."

There were nods all around. Wanda sat back in her chair and folded her arms over her chest. Her hands were rough and worn from years of work. "Maybe that's what we should call ourselves—The Cafe of Misfit Women."

The others chuckled, but then grew silent. Perhaps they were all thinking, like Melanie was, how tough it was to pursue something new among people who didn't understand you.

In a moment of rare honesty, she blurted out, "I'm not happy with what I'm doing, but I'm afraid of what others will think if I go for something more. Afraid they'll say I'm thinking too highly of myself. Over-reaching and trying to be somebody I'm not."

The women nodded.

"I'm afraid everyone thinks I'm a terrible mother." Julia's leg stopped bouncing for a moment. "That I'm being selfish and greedy, sacrificing their well-being for my dream, when I should be focused on my home and family right now."

The confessions were rolling now. Gabrielle sat forward. "You both are scaring me. You're already farther along in this process than me, and my biggest hope is that things will get better. I'm afraid I'll be stuck working for the florist forever, and never get anywhere. I can't be satisfied there, but it sounds like living my dream isn't such a great thing either."

Wanda snorted. "Trust me, honey, I've been 'living the dream' for nearly thirty years. It only gets harder. You want to know my fear? I'm afraid if I don't get out, and soon, I'm going to crash and burn."

After a moment of silence, Julia breathed out a heavy sigh. "And there's something else... Underneath it all, I have this nagging feeling that none of it has any value. That nothing I'm doing has any real purpose. That it makes no difference in the world, except maybe to make a good income for my family someday. I feel like God gave me these gifts and abilities, and I'm trying to use them, but I'm not sure I'm doing the right things or that any of it matters."

"Maybe we *should* be doing other things." Melanie squeezed Julia's shoulder because the woman looked close to tears. "Maybe all of this dream-chasing *is* selfish and worthless. I mean, a lot of women would say it is. Would say we should be putting all our energy toward our kids—" She stopped herself, since Gabrielle wasn't even married yet, and Wanda's kids were adults long ago. She started again. "Seasons of life, like they say..." But she didn't have any real answers. What season of life were Gabrielle and Wanda experiencing, thirty years apart and on opposite ends of the child-rearing spectrum? The only people who ever talked about "seasons of life" were the ones who felt stuck in the kid-phase and were trying to encourage themselves that it wouldn't last forever. Besides, even if she gave up the theater for more time with her seventeen-year-old, she'd still have her office job. And her son was rarely ever around the house anyway.

The silence had lengthened, with each of them lost in their own thoughts. No one even responded to her comments. An air of sadness, with perhaps a bit of shame and guilt mixed in, lay heavy on them all.

It was the young and energetic Gabrielle who spoke first.

She leaned forward, slapped a hand on the shiny black table and trained her dark eyes on each of them. "So, how are we going to figure this out?"

3

impactivity beats productivity

Each of the women in the "Cafe of Misfit Women" would be considered productive. Successful, even.

Julia owns her own cafe and from the sounds of those chocolate peanut butter brownies, it's thriving. Melanie has both an administrative job and a volunteer position. Wanda has raised a family to adulthood all while running a successful business. And Gabrielle acts far different from many young women her age—she has a full-time job and big dreams.

Anyone watching these women from the outside would call them productive.

But are they having an impact? Maybe not.

Like the "misfit women," many of us know how to be productive. We get our to-dos done and still have time to add a few more and cross them off, too.

Impactivity takes more, though.

is work/life balance even possible?

Everywhere I go, people say that they are too busy. "Not enough time" is the mantra of our information- and opportunity-deluged society. We want more rest, more time off, more vacation days, more sleeping in, but we can't seem to get off the treadmill.

I would suggest to you that we don't actually want more rest. That we are not too busy. What we truly want when we say "less busy" is to be less frantic. We want to be busy *with purpose and intent*. And what we truly want when we say "more rest" is more peace. In other words, you want to be purposeful and peaceful, but you settle for periods of confused and frantic activity, alternated with periods of distracting and numbing leisure. We run and run and then we crash. If this description fits you, I believe God wants to talk to you about your heart first, not about your schedule.

I resist the concept of "work/life balance" that is so often spoken of today. It implies that work is the opposite of life. As if life is what happens when you are not working. But what generally happens when you are not working? Sleep. Television. Errands. Is this how you define "life"? Or do you think of "life" as something more vaguely resembling a hammock on a tropical island? I would suggest that you stop thinking of work as something to get through so you can get to your real goal of living. Because living rarely comes in the way you define it. It's fleeting and short-lived.

Think of it this way: If you spend fifteen hours a week "really living," during the sixty years of your adult life those hours add up to a little over five years. Even if you take out eight hours of sleep, it's only eight years of waking time spent "living." And most of us probably don't come close to fifteen hours a week of this ill-defined, non-work "life."

You need a new perspective.

You need to *live* while you work.

You need to *rest* in a way that recovers your energy.

You need **work/rest** balance.

But not work/life balance.

By now, you've probably noticed that balance isn't one of the six elements of Impactivity. It's more of the undergirding, the foundation. But you must understand that a balanced life has nothing to do with the amount of minutes spent in varying activities. There will always be more work than rest (just like your waking time is usually double your sleeping time). Perhaps you tend to define balance in the sense of the importance you place on areas of your life or the priority they take, but what does that even mean? How do you assign importance or priority except with the time you spend or the order in which you do things?

Balance implies two equally-weighted elements, whether in time, importance, or something else. This visual picture is of little use, because you rarely even picture only two things. At the very least you will name physical, spiritual, mental/emotional, and relational health. Or work, school, people, fun, home, exercise. You talk about being well-rounded. You have so many things going on in your life, you are more likely to picture a number of plates spinning at once. Plate-spinning is a very different mental image than a balanced scale. Plate-spinning is frantic and stressful. But balance doesn't make sense either.

We clearly need a new metaphor.

life is a highway

At the risk of getting a tune stuck in your head, life is a highway. When you're on the highway, you're meant to be moving. Some days are left-lane fast and some days are right-lane slow. If you're always veering out to drive on the left shoulder so you can pass everyone, you're going too fast. Either there's a life-and-death emergency, or you're a crazy person. If you're going so slowly in the right lane that you end up pulling over and stopping on the shoulder, then something is also wrong. Either there's a malfunction, or you need to sleep. It's natural and right to shift between left and right lanes, but shoulder-driving means something needs to change.

The place where work ends and rest begins will change day by day, through seasons of life and age, health and circumstances. There is no right or wrong place for work to end and rest to begin, no right time for the slow lane or the passing lane. There is only "not enough" and "too much" of either one. When you veer into the left shoulder of too much work, it's because you've left joy and entered striving. When you roll to a stop on the right shoulder of too much rest, it's usually because you are fearful. If you have true joy and no striving in your work, you're rarely tempted to rest longer than necessary. And when the joyful work exhausts you, you know you need to rest.

Of course, like on any highway, there are always rest stops. Holidays, vacations, family gatherings, pit stops, if you will.

34

They are there for refueling, for rejuvenating, for stretching your legs. As long as we live and are still "driving," rest stops are critical. (It may help to imagine every rest stop a beautiful park, instead of an Exxon and a Starbucks.) How often you make use of the rest stops is between you and God. There is no right amount of rest-stopping. But there is certainly a wrong amount. If you are driving until you pass out from hunger, or your car runs out of gas, or you fall asleep at the wheel, clearly you did too much driving and not enough resting. At some point your driving lost its joy, because joyful driving allows for times to eat and sleep and refuel. Only frantic, deadline-pressured driving doesn't stop for these natural needs.

There can be too much resting. You pull over for a needed break or refueling, and then you never get back on the highway, even after you're rested and refueled. Why would anyone do that? Perhaps it's fear. Fear of highway conditions or other drivers or even your destination. We'll tackle those fears in chapters to come.

Finding the right speed (and strategy) to navigate the highway of life takes discipline. And listening. You may need some temporary rules for yourself about when to make the shift (stop working at a certain time, start working at a certain time) to ensure you're getting enough rest but not too much. You will certainly need prayer and time for reflection. And you most definitely will need the fortitude it takes to make mistakes and get right back on the road.

Perfect balance is a myth. It's not going to happen. Let it go. You can make an idol out of balance and feel discontent at anything short of it. No one is weighing your minutes, your priorities, or your sleep. Instead of balance, in the pages to come you're going to learn a life of healthy forward-progress, quick course-correction to avoid disaster, and plenty of time to enjoy the scenery as you travel down the highway on the journey of a lifetime. Instead of feeling pressured to feel balanced, perhaps *thriving* is a better word choice.

what is impactivity?

Impactivity is the distinction between the mere productivity you strive for and the deeper impact that you wish to have in the world. This deeper impact is difficult to measure, to quantify, even difficult to define, and so you settle for something less—a life that is busy and full of task completion, with little time for ruminating over its possible pointlessness. If the goal and desire is to live a fruitful life, then productivity is the leafiness that disguises a fruitless vine. In other words, the vine of your life is super-productive, shooting out leaves in every direction, looking green and glossy and healthy, growing full and tall and impressive. But there is little fruit.

It takes humility to admit that some of your achievements may have been "fruitless," in other words, of little value except to look pretty or impressive. How many of us settle for leafiness instead of fruitfulness? For productivity instead of Impactivity?

Impactivity is productivity plus purpose. It is a whole-life plan for healthy kingdom-building that brings joy, not stress. Impactivity sometimes prunes away the beautifully productive leaves to give more growth to the withering fruit. It is a life that is not only productive, but is also world-changing, world-impacting, because it is lived out of a place of freedom, clarity,

36

and renewed energy.

So where does the fruit of Impactivity come from? How do you get there?

First, this book assumes you have a relationship with the True Vine. In John 15, Jesus explains this metaphor of Himself as the Vine and His followers as the branches, who must stay connected to bear fruit. "Apart from me you can do nothing," Jesus says. Before Impactivity can begin, you understand your place as a branch that must cling to that Vine, abiding in Him as not only the *source* of all fruit, but the *reason* for bearing it.

Even so, you must also understand that your exhausted striving does not serve the world in the way God desires. You have a calling, an adventure, a quest that only you can undertake. That far-off place calls to you, and you must understand it, develop a vision and embrace the **dream** of it.

There will be hindrances pulling you back. Chains around your ankles that would keep you living just as you are now and subvert your adventure. Before you can begin your quest, you must get **unshackled** of all that would stop you from pursuing it.

But the dream and the freedom are not enough. You must also strive for the clarity of a **design**, a plan that maps out the adventure you are about to undertake. You must understand how to **ignite** your passion, to push through the mundane days, the overwhelming details, the myriad of distractions.

You must learn how to rest. How to **recharge** your physical, emotional, and spiritual energy to get back to the quest with joy. And you must understand the need to **connect** with others who will share in your Dream and keep you accountable.

These six bold words are the **Six Elements of Impactivity**, and all of them are necessary for a life that is more than productive – one that makes a lasting impact.

That's what you want, isn't it? If your life is only about productivity, and not about a deeper purpose behind the productivity, then you are simply chasing the wind. Or you are self-indulgent, striving only to build up your own image and ego.

Only Impactivity has any real meaning.

And only Impactivity leads you to the kingdom-building possibilities that God has in store for you.

journal

_____

_____

_____

_____

_____

_____

_____

_____

_____

_____

_____

_____

_____

_____

4

misfits

Julia's Java Bean Cafe was once again hosting Gabrielle, Melanie, and Wanda after hours, but tonight the four women buzzed excitedly about the guest still to arrive.

Since the last time they met, a woman's name had popped into Melanie's mind. Her friend Stef had always said that her mother Victoria was the epitome of a successful and put-together business woman. Melanie had gotten in touch with Victoria through Stef, and the older woman had agreed to meet with the four at the Cafe of Misfit Women, as they were now calling their gathering.

"I told her 5:30." Melanie sipped her pumpkin spice latte, then smiled at Julia in gratitude for the brew. "I wanted to give us a half-hour to think of questions."

Gabrielle leaned forward, pen poised over a notebook.

"What did you say her business was?"

"I'm not exactly sure. I feel like Stef's always mentioning different things her mother's doing—or has done. She's definitely been successful in business, I know that. Done a lot of traveling and speaking, I think. Maybe written a book? I think there was a non-profit organization in there somewhere."

"Wow." Julia sighed. "I can barely get my hair brushed in the morning and still run this cafe."

They spent a few minutes talking over the things they wanted to ask Victoria. They were all hoping for a healthy list of some tips and tricks on productivity and balance. Surely a woman who had done so much could teach them about how to live like they desired. Gabrielle was ready with her notebook, planning to take copious notes and then distribute them to the other women after tonight. Wanda had her doubts that any of it would help, but she was willing to listen.

Victoria arrived promptly at five thirty, gliding through the door so gently the bell above it barely jangled. She was tall, with stylishly short cropped salt-and-pepper hair. She wore a black and white wool hounds tooth jacket and a white silk scarf, and silver hoops glittered at her ears. Melanie jumped up and made quick introductions, and Victoria reached to shake each of their hands firmly, smiling brightly at every woman.

"Please, sit." Julia extended a hand to the chair at the head of their table. "Can I get you an espresso?"

Victoria smiled. "Not at this hour, I'm afraid. I'd be awake until Wednesday. I'd love a glass of water with lemon."

Julia bounced away to get the water, and was back thirty seconds later to set the water on the table.

Victoria sat erect in her chair, hands folded together on the table. "So, what can I do for you lovely ladies?"

The three looked to Melanie, who had somehow become the unofficial leader of their clan. She took a deep breath and launched in, giving Victoria a quick summary of how they'd come together, their mutual frustrations, and the hope that Victoria could give them some advice... specifically about how to escape the constant feeling of being overwhelmed and exhausted all the time and how to feel more productive and balanced.

The older woman listened silently through Melanie's rush of words, nodded and smiled a few times, and then when Melanie rambled to a stop, surveyed each of them in turn. "Why don't you each tell me a little about your business and personal lives."

It took close to thirty minutes for the four of them to spill out the highs and lows of their work, their home lives, and the uncertain nature of their futures. Victoria listened to each with her full attention, seemingly in no hurry.

While the others talked and Victoria listened, Melanie observed.

Perhaps it was simply Victoria's classy clothing and jewelry, which Melanie especially admired, but she seemed wealthy. She was clearly relaxed, despite their near-desperate begging for her advice. She had the sort of serene, knowing smile that waits quietly and patiently to be heard. It was also hard to tell her age. Since she was Stef's mother, she had to be at least sixty-five, perhaps older. She looked incredibly healthy. Vibrant, even. In many ways she seemed younger than Wanda.

It was Wanda who was last to give the details of her life, spilling out a woeful tale of overwork and annoyance in the restaurant business and her hope to be rid of all of it soon, selling the restaurant and going back to the simple catering that had started it all.

When she had finished, they all looked to Victoria at the head of the table, as though she would wave a magic wand and turn the rags of their hopes and dreams into ball gowns.

Elbows on the polished wood and fingers steepled together, Victoria took her time before speaking. Her expression had turned sober. "First of all, we must make an agreement if I am to give you any sort of advice."

They all nodded, willing at this point to agree to nearly anything.

"Never again—and I do mean *never*—will you refer to this place as the Cafe of Misfit Women."

All the women were startled.

Victoria continued. "I see before me a group of four driven, energetic—albeit tired—women who have been given gifts, skills, abilities, and opportunities to do great things. A 'misfit' implies something broken or damaged, that something is fundamentally wrong with you. You may be different, but it is your *rarity* that makes you incredibly valuable to the world. You are not misfits. Are we perfectly clear?"

Julia was grinning at Melanie. "I like this chick."

"However," Victoria again commanded their attention, "and it is a big 'however'—you are each drowning in self-doubt, confusion, disorganization, and exhaustion. It's time for each of you to wake up. You are not serving the world this way. God has more in mind for you, and He has made you for more."

Something loosened inside Melanie in that moment. Some of the ever-present tension drained from her neck and

44

shoulders. She looked at the table to hide the emotion in her eyes at Victoria's words of both blessing and challenge. She became suddenly aware of the lovely smell of pumpkin spice, the soft saxophone and snare drum easing from the speakers overhead, the cozy warmth of the fireplace. It was like being given a glimpse of a far-off castle and a promise that you were headed for that adventure. Perhaps Victoria really was a fairy godmother.

Wanda cleared her throat. "So how do we get there?"

Victoria smiled. "Now you are asking the right question. But the answer would take more time than we have this evening, I'm afraid. I would say that there are six elements each of you needs to embrace to begin fully living your adventure." She looked at Gabrielle's bright and eager smile. "It's never too early to implement these principles." Her gaze shifted to Wanda's slumped posture. "Neither is it ever too late."

Julia rubbed at her forehead. "I'll be honest. I don't think I have the time for a single thing, let alone six."

Victoria studied her. "All the more reason you need them."

Gabrielle was still holding her pen. "Can you just give us a few tips? I'll write down the six steps, and maybe we can work on them in the weeks to come?"

Victoria sipped her lemon water, as if carefully considering her next words. "I'll tell you what." Her gaze took in all four of them. "I will meet you here every Monday at 5:30 for the next six weeks and share with you the road to Impactivity."

"Impact-what?" Gabrielle was scribbling, but had gotten stuck.

Victoria laughed, a light and musical sound. "Impactivity. Like *productivity* but with more impact."

There were eager nods all around, and Melanie guessed that each of them had glimpsed in Victoria's words a personal promise of relief, like she had.

"I must warn you, though." Victoria said. "It will not be easy. There will be work."

They all paused, listening intently.

She smiled at each of them. "Get ready for the journey of a lifetime!" In the beat of silence that followed, Victoria picked up a pastry and bit into it. "This is delicious!"

impactivity.com

part two

the six elements of impactivity

5

dream
glimpse the horizon

The Lord God took the man and put him in the
garden of Eden to work it and keep it.
Genesis 2:15

T he mere fact that you are reading this book tells me that
you have a dream.

It may be hidden in the far reaches of your heart, covered
up, stuffed aside, put away for so long that you hardly
remember it.

But it's there.

And there is a part of you that has always been whispering
your Dream.

listen to your dream

Your dream is hardly a mystery.

Chances are the secret has made itself known in various ways, even if you haven't pursued it, even if you've run from it. It's the ending of the sentence, "I've always loved..." Or maybe, "I've always wished I could..." Before you can live a life of true Impactivity, you must get in touch with this (perhaps buried) part of yourself and ask it some questions.

I had a dream that started at the age of eight. It was audacious, but I didn't know it at the time because I was eight. I was going to write a novel. This dream was big enough in my heart even then that I vividly remember the *exact* moment I wrote the first sentence. I was in the backseat of my parents' car, at a gas station just off the interstate, about to begin a family trip to New York City. For years, and I mean *years,* afterward, I thought about that novel every single time we passed that gas station. It was a dream that took twenty-six years to be realized.

Are you afraid? Fear always follows in the wake of a big dream. The bigger the dream, the bigger the fear. Perhaps you fear that admitting your dream and then not realizing it will crush you. Or you fear that you don't have what it takes. Or that you'll be blocked by your circumstances. All these fears may be legitimate.

Does it feel wrong to admit your discontent? Give yourself some time to go there. It's not wrong to examine your life and see where it's lacking, especially if it drives growth.

How about your embarrassment or hesitation over dreaming big? Do you tend to downplay or even keep silent about the future you wish you could pursue or the lofty goals you are currently chasing? Perhaps you've shared some of this with someone in the past, and then been shamed or told you are unrealistic. Spend some time on this—it's only you and me here. Give yourself a chance to envision a future you would love to experience. This is not a selfish exercise. This is an experiment in thought, to explore the adventure where God might be leading you. A big Adventure with a capital A. You have an Adventure before you. Where do you want it to lead? Thing big. Think crazy. Think unrealistic.

For now, don't let them stop you from thinking through, and even writing down your great big dreams. Do it.

Ok, now that you've listened to yourself (and to me), it's time to listen to God.

For we are his workmanship, created in Christ Jesus for good works, which God prepared beforehand, that we should walk in them.
Ephesians 2:10-11

All those dreams, those loves you heard while listening to yourself—you must understand that everything you are, everything that has happened to you, everything you dream about, all these things have been allowed to shape you and been orchestrated by God as preparation and part of the Adventure of your life. Do you think that while God was crafting the workmanship of *you*, He forgot to think about the good works He was preparing for you to *do*? Those dreams and longings are not something that developed in secret and unknown places inside you that are better left untouched. They are part of you for a reason.

I hope you grasp that all your interior longings and desires for impact, to live large in your world and make a difference, have been placed inside you by God. His intention is to motivate you into fulfilling the Adventure He has planned for you. By denying this dream, this Adventure, out of any kind of fear or shame or guilt, you are actually denying God's call on your life.

Your dream may involve going further in your current job or business or ministry. It may be an entirely different direction, creating a new business or following a new creative pursuit or serving in a new way. No matter where you are right now in your life, there is more Adventure calling out to you. The work of our hands and the good purposes of God in our life were established all the way back in the first Garden. If you are still alive, you have not arrived.

The *more* of your Adventure may be fuzzy and vague at this point. Don't worry, there is more discovering to be done.

discover your dream

Not only are your inner desires for Adventure a clue to the dream you should have for your life, but also the skills, abilities and gifts you've been given. Who are you? Where are all the places where you shine? The ways you excel? The skills people seek out in you and the gifts you're praised for?

Make a list of all your strengths. All your assets. Can you play an instrument? Write it down. A champion horseshoe thrower? Write it down. I mean it. Everything! No one is going to read it, so give yourself the space to brag a little.

Now make another list, this time a list of everything you

are passionate about. All the individuals and groups of people and segments of the population that you care deeply about. All the causes that fire your blood. All the material things you highly value. All the activities you love to participate in—perhaps a hobby or a side job. Maybe part or all of your current profession. Maybe something you haven't done in a very long time but that still draws your heart.

You don't need to do this all at once if it feels like pressure. Take your time. Some of the items on list number two will feel like overlap with the first list, but that's actually the point. In fact, when you are done with that second list, go through and circle the items on both lists that overlap. In other words, circle the skills, abilities and gifts you possess that allow you to do something very well that you also happen to love doing and/or care passionately about. Do you see where I'm going here?

Now, let's think about what you have to offer to others. Those circled items represent the "sweet spot" for you. If you've been diligent to write down everything you could think of on those two lists, then I am positive that somewhere embedded in there is the key to the Adventure you are meant to live.

One important note: often we believe that for our lives to matter, our particular adventures must be centered around sharing the gospel or some other officially-recognized "ministry" activity. Can we, for example, live a life of Impactivity centered around generating financial success? How about centered around a creative pursuit that does not have an explicit "Jesus" message? (If you're going to be a sculptor, can you only sculpt religious statues?) I would suggest that all work,

since the first job of tending the Garden was handed out, has
been sacred. The world-change that can be effected through
people with wealth requires people to earn wealth. Beauty that
follows in the footsteps of the Great Creator requires creative
artists. Your work, your calling, no matter what it is, has an
inherently sacred quality.

But God-given Adventures are about much more than
self-gratification in the form of job enjoyment, success, or
income, aren't they? God-given Adventures are about offering
yourself in love to others, connecting your true self with the
deeper needs around you, to be part of the building of God's
kingdom, which has already begun.

If your dream involves owning a business, then the gifts
and skills you are able to offer others are what they will find
valuable and where they will be willing to pay for your
expertise, excellent service, or talent.

For clarity, picture the three intersecting circles of a Venn
diagram. Circle #1 represents all your gifts, skills, and abilities.
Circle #2 contains all the things you care deeply about. In
Circle #3 is where you would list the needs of the world that
you see. Where those three circles intersect, everything they
have in common is the key to the Adventure you could be (and
probably should be) living.

Your Dream may take you into a large company, it may
involve creating a small business, or it may never leave your
home. The scope and the potential for income are of very little
consequence here. What matters is that you connect your
Dream to your deeper purpose.

understand the obstacles

No dream is easy.

And I can all but guarantee that you will face many internal and external obstacles to overcome in the pursuit of your dream, in the living out of your Adventure.

But some of the biggest obstacles you are going to face must be overcome before you can even begin.

Your own fear of failure is a huge obstacle. It keeps you waiting for permission to begin, asking others for their opinions, gathering more information—all stalling tactics, really. You want guarantees that you won't fail, and you don't even want to start until you're certain everything is perfectly aligned for your success.

News flash: Perfection is not going to happen. If you keep waiting for it, you will never start. We are going to talk more about this fear in the pages to come, but I will say here that being a true "perfectionist"—feeling that everything you do has to be flawless and you cannot risk failure—is usually a euphemism for a person who is in bondage to others' opinions.

Another obstacle may be guilt. You feel guilty for pursuing something so audacious. Who are you to make so much of yourself? And you feel bad that your success can make others' failure stand in sharp relief and cause them to feel shame or resentment. You think it might be better to stay small.

And then there are the lies you believe. Some of them come from others, some come from within yourself, and I truly believe that some of them come from our enemy, who would go to any length to keep you from pursuing your calling.

You don't have it what it takes.
You're not smart enough,
Lucky enough.
You don't have the resources.

Lies, all of them.

It is prideful to stand out in the crowd.
You should hide those gifts.

More lies.

It's wrong to make money.

It's wrong for a woman to have pursuits outside of her family, or for a man to prioritize something that doesn't earn money.

Examine these statements closely, because they are tricky.

Even when you clear out all these internal obstacles, you are still left with the external circumstances of your life that seem to prevent any kind of Adventure from getting underway. It seems impossible to tackle, given your busy life and level of exhaustion. The dream is big and scary and you have no idea where to begin or how to incorporate it into your life. You need to make income in other, safer ways. When it comes down to it, you believe you don't have the time, or you don't have the money, or you don't have the energy to make your dream a reality.

I don't scoff at any of these obstacles. I don't tell you that they are weak excuses (although they may be). I only say this: If you are convinced that God has gifted you for a particular work, and that He has also given you a passion for it, and it is a gift that meets a need in the world, then I think God will show you how to find the time, money, and energy to live in obedience.

We will talk more about getting free of lies and obstacles

as we move into the second element of Impactivity: Unshackle. For now, start thinking through your obstacles and dismantling them as best you can.

commit to pursuit

We've listened to ourselves and God, discovered our unique Adventure in the world, and taken notice of some of the preliminary obstacles. Now what is it going to look like to pursue this dream? Again, there is so much more to come as we create a vision and strategy for your Adventure. But here's a sneak preview:

You're going to find the time. You're going to pull it from other places, plug the leaks you didn't realize you had, and learn ways to multiply it.

You're going to take some risks. You're going to get brave enough to step into things that only God can help you accomplish, creating an urgent need for God to show up in your life.

You're going to cultivate a growth mindset. Rather than believing that your situation is fixed, you are going to embrace the idea of learning and pushing forward, expecting some failure and even welcoming it as a key to learning and growing.

To Dream is to understand yourself and your place in the world. The Dream is the far-off destination, which you recognize is fuzzy and vague and may change, but it's what will pull you along the journey.

It's what you imagine at the horizon.

The journey itself is the Adventure. It will take unexpected twists and have ups and downs, and the place you reach may look nothing like what you are imagining, but still this quest is always guided by the Dream you have envisioned. Likely when you arrive, you will find that the horizon is no closer—there is another Adventure to be had. This is why no matter where you are in life, there is more Adventure to come. Perhaps you're in one of the sequels already. *The Adventure Returns*.

Once you've understood the Adventure and have committed to undertaking it, the rest of the journey toward Impactivity requires making the most of those gifts through training and learning, and then putting them to maximum use. These last two, the maximizing of your gifts and the releasing of them where they can be utilized to the fullest, are what the rest of this book is about.

Maximizing and releasing.

It's going to be fun!

journal

_____

_____

_____

_____

_____

_____

_____

_____

_____

_____

_____

_____

_____

_____

6

week one: the dreaming

Each of the women at the Java Bean Cafe sat hunched over her own notebook around one of Julia's larger tables. Gabrielle finished her assignment first and laid her pen down quietly. She met Victoria's quiet smile with one of her own, and felt the woman's approval, even though Gabrielle had not yet shared the way her different lists had come together to start to reveal something new about her dream.

One by one, each of them finished and looked up from their notebooks, with Wanda the last one scribbling with her work-worn hands.

"That wasn't an easy assignment, Victoria." Melanie's beaded bracelet clinked against the table as she stretched out her fingers.

"If it were easy it would not be so vital, my dear."

Gabrielle smiled at Victoria's typical no-nonsense response. The woman had given them much to think about in the area of dreaming, and then set them to writing lists of their gifts and skills, their passions, and the places where they saw need in their world. "I've never really thought about it like that," she said. "About what the world needs, I mean. I've always loved weddings. I think it's what drew me to start working for a florist in high school. And I knew I'd make a good wedding planner, because I'm naturally organized and detail oriented. But I meet lots of wedding planners in the floral shop, and they all work super hard to make a decent living. My plan has been to start a wedding coordination *company*, so that I could have others working for me and have some freedom. I've never given any real thought to what the world needed from me, though. And I have to say, I'm still not entirely sure I get it."

Victoria cocked her head to the side and studied Gabrielle. "Perhaps you have not yet gone deep enough. Tell me why you are passionate about wedding coordination."

Gabrielle took a breath to speak, but then laughed and shrugged. "You'll think it sounds—" She stopped at the firm raise of Victoria's hand, cutting off her sentence.

"No. We will not allow you to be embarrassed by your passion or to make excuses for what you care about, dear Gabrielle. Not here. Tell us why you are passionate about wedding coordination."

Gabrielle bit her lip, but then nodded and took the plunge. "I was the flower girl in a wedding when I was six. An older cousin getting married. I was so thrilled to be part of it, and felt like a fairy tale princess in my flower girl dress. The whole thing was so beautiful, from the flowers to the clothes, the music and the food. Everything, that is, except my cousin. She was a mess from the start of the day, and probably before. Crying one minute and yelling at her mother or bridesmaids the next. At the time, she seemed like the wicked witch of the fairy tale to me, but as I got older and remembered, I knew that she had simply been stressed with all the details of the day beyond her ability to cope. I always felt so sad, that what should have been a day of joy was so difficult for her." Gabrielle forced herself to meet the eyes of her friends. "It seems silly that such a small thing would have had such a profound impact on me, but somewhere along the way I vowed that I would never let a bride feel that way if I could help her."

Victoria was leaning forward, elbows on the table and long-fingered hands tucked under her chin. "Why not?"

"Because a wedding is so important. It's the sacred joining of two lives forever, and I believe in marriage, in the way it undergirds society and gives people the security to move forward in their lives. I want to have a small part in making it sacred, not stressful. I want to make it easy for brides to focus on the important step they are taking, not whether the details are right." She finished, a little breathless from the unexpected surge of excitement her statement had brought.

"Ah, there we have it." Victoria smiled. "You have found your deeper *Why*. The reason behind your dream and calling. This is the connection to loving others and the service you can perform in the world. You want to train your wedding planners to each take their duties as seriously as you do."

Gabrielle sat back in her chair, pleased. "Yes, that's it

exactly. I just—I just never thought of it that way before."

"What was your dream, Victoria?" Julia asked. was tapping her pen on her notebook in a rhythmic beat, probably unaware she was even doing it.

The older woman still wore black and white tonight, this time with a splash of red jewelry at her throat and wrists, and on her elegantly-painted fingernails. She waved away the question with a delicate hand. "Oh, I've had several dreams over the years, and more that have come true than I would have dared to dream. But tonight is about the four of you." She turned to Wanda and pointed to her notebook. "Tell us what you've been working on there."

Wanda shrugged a shoulder and put an arm over her writing. "Doesn't matter. I'm much too old for dreaming."

"Ha!" Victoria's sharp laugh startled them all. "If you are too old, then I may as well call it a day." She patted Wanda's hand, then pulled it gently away from her notebook. "We must dream until the day we wake up, Wanda. Wake up on the other side, where we do not yet know how the dreaming will work. You are not too old."

Wanda shifted uncomfortably. "Fine. But I don't know how to make sense of it. I've always been interested in cooking, of course. And I care about lots of people. I don't know how that all fits together in some kind of dream, other than the dream-turned-nightmare I'm already living."

Victoria nodded. "Tell me why you are passionate about cooking."

"It's not the cooking so much, I guess. It's more the way that food makes people happy, makes them feel taken care of."

"You like taking care of people?"

"Yeah. I guess I do. Yes. I like making them feel... loved."

Gabrielle watched the smiles around the table. Considering Wanda's usual grumpiness, it was a surprising revelation. Perhaps the grumpiness came from her circumstances more than her heart.

"Who do you want to feel loved, Wanda?" Victoria gave her an encouraging smile.

"Lots of people. My family, of course. My customers in the restaurant. And..."

"Yes?"

Wanda sighed. "Well, there is this other thing. Something that's been bothering me for a few years now, but I don't know what to do about it."

Victoria's raised eyebrows were her only response. The rest of them waited, too.

"It's the homeless people that wait in the alley behind the restaurant every night for something to eat. They used to wait in the shadows for the busboys or kitchen staff to throw bags of food in the dumpster. But some of my employees were complaining because the homeless guys freaked them out."

"So something changed?"

Wanda folded her arms over her chest. "Yeah, I couldn't stand the thought of them digging through garbage for their dinner. Not when I had a whole restaurant of perfectly good food in there. So I started making up take-out containers at the end of the night with all the food we had left over. Eventually it wasn't enough so I had the chef always make extra so we'd have enough for those who knew to come."

Victoria laughed quietly. "Wanda, you are running a soup kitchen out the back of your restaurant?"

"I wouldn't exactly call it—"

"What do you think, ladies?" The older woman's eyes sparkled. "Does Wanda still have some work to do on discovering the next part of the Adventure of her life?"

Gabrielle watched the expression on Wanda's face as it went from confusion, to wide-eyed fear, to an incredulous but shy smile.

Maybe there was something to this dreaming thing after all.

dream summary

listen to your dream

- Listen to your lifelong dreams
- Refuse embarrassment, guilt, and shame
- Hear the call of God to your great Adventure

discover your dream

- Uncover your amazing skills and gifts
- Identify your passion for people and ideas
- Pinpoint what the world needs

understand the obstacles

- Overcome the fear of failure that holds you back
- Feel no guilt about dreaming big
- Uncover the lies that shackle you
- Find the time, money, and energy to pursue your Dream

commit to pursuit

- Create regular time to work on your Dream
- Face risks with courage
- Cultivate a growth and learning mindset

For a beautiful PDF Guide featuring a summary of the Impactivity elements, suitable for printing and reference, please visit impactivity.com/six-elements.

7

unshackle
find freedom

For you were called to freedom, brothers.
Only do not use your freedom as an opportunity for the flesh,
but through love serve one another.
Galatians 5:13

How is possible to pursue a Dream and still remain healthy and sane? You have so much going on in your life already, how can you possibly add another thing?

The answer is, you probably can't. Not without subtracting first. But the process of unshackling yourself from all the things that hinder you from pursuing your Adventure is more than just a process of clearing out the obvious and tangible busyness in your life. It's a *spiritual* process first. It's coming to a place of understanding about the spiritual roots of what is keeping you shackled.

For me, this process began with a very innocent question from my mother-in-law. At a holiday family gathering, she once asked me, "Have you been really busy this month?" I answered, "I'm *always* busy." And then I went off by myself and thought, *Yes, I am always busy. Always. Too busy. Something is wrong.*

It took time and more intense circumstances for me to begin understanding what was wrong. I began to realize that I had elevated work and productivity to an unhealthy status in my heart, to a place of worship, really. But I still had deeper work to do, to figure out *why* I had made achieving so important, and how I could possibly stop.

escape the shackles

You can't pursue your Adventure until you've figured out a way to eliminate all the detours and side trips from your road. And this can be hard. Some of these things have been part of your drive for years—meaningless jobs, hobbies that don't bring fulfillment, even people who drag you away from your calling.

But only by escaping the shackles will you be able to find the Adventure that God has called you to. Here are a few of the things that may be holding you back from Impactivity:

misinterpreting your identity

Impactivity requires freedom, and one of the most common forms of bondage we face stems from our identity. Or mis-identity, if you will.

Our identity is where we really need to do the hard spiritual work. The truth is that every one of us wants to be loved and admired, and very often we construct our entire lives around this goal. We derive our identity from the way that other people see us. If they love us and admire us, we feel good about ourselves. And so much of what we do in life is designed to either 1) please people to get them to love us or 2) impress people to get them to admire us.

Take a moment with that truth.

Is that really why God created you to dream, to live, to Adventure? No, it's not. One of the biggest shackles that holds us back from Impactivity is the desire to please others instead of the One who created us to make an impact. So the first shackle that I ask you to unlock as you begin this journey is to carefully and prayerfully consider your identity in Him. Not in your activities, or the way you are seen in your community or your family. Not in your mind, but in Him.

Our identity can only come from one place if we want to actually pursue our Adventure and live a life of Impactivity. From the way God sees us. Not from the way other people see us. And the way God sees us is very different from the way that other people do. It's hard to see ourselves through God's eyes. It seems like humility to say, "God couldn't possibly love me because I'm such a mess." But that statement is not humility. You are placing your own mess above God's ability to wipe it away and use you in the way that He desires. Your identity must be rooted in His unconditional love and acceptance. When God says He loves you just as you are, there's no qualifier at the end of that sentence.

Why is this so difficult for us? Why do we feel the need to

tracy higley

please and impress *even God* to gain His love and his acceptance? Isn't that what we're often doing? We may insist that our serving, working hard, and burning ourselves out is in service to God, but aren't we often trying to solidify our identity by making ourselves pleasing and impressive to God Himself? To earn His favor?

Do you think it's working? Or do you believe that God already loved you before you accomplished anything? Do you believe that God has chosen to fully accept you because He has already paid the price needed for His favor to be granted?

other people's adventures

Here's the problem: in the same way that you have an Adventure to pursue, a Dream that God has gifted you *with* and gifted you *for*, so does everyone else. I call these "Other People's Adventures" (OPA). And if you're not careful, others will start shackling you to their adventures and enlisting you to get their work done. Please understand that I'm not saying there's anything wrong with serving or helping other people. We all need each other to live out our calling. What I am saying is that if your desire to be loved and admired to feel good about yourself is driving you to make choices you would not make otherwise, then your involvement in OPA is keeping you from living your own Adventure.

You cannot live a life of Impactivity until you let go of all the ways in which you've committed to OPA to give you identity. It's not that helping others on their adventures is bad, but simply that you can't let OPA lead you away from your own Adventure. And you can't let the Dream that God set on someone else's heart steal *your* Dream.

72

impactivity.com

When we misplace our identity in others' opinions of us, it feels necessary to say yes to everyone else's pull on us. We stay shackled to others' adventures (with a lowercase "a") and pack our calendars to overflowing, missing out on our true Adventure.

too much stuff

There is another area where we need freedom before we can move forward in Impactivity. And just as the fear of being unloved and worthless keeps us shackled to pleasing and performing for people, there is a fear behind this form of shackling, too. The fear of being in need keeps us in bondage to the *stuff* in our lives. The choices we make to accumulate, to display, to put in storage, and to hoard keep us locked in a mental prison of overwhelm. When the physical space around you is cluttered and you never feel like you're on top of all the organizational projects that need doing, how can you possibly feel free to pursue a new Adventure?

But as I said, getting unshackled is about more than the tangible acts of clearing out our calendars or our clutter. There is a very deep spiritual issue at work here, too. It's the issue of trust. It is no coincidence that Jesus directly followed his words about the dangers of serving both God and money with the reassurance that in seeking first His kingdom, all the rest of our needs would be given to us. I can almost hear his listeners muttering, "Sure, it's all well and good for you to tell us we can't serve God and be focused on money. You're practically homeless. But we have to take care of our families. Put a roof over our heads and food in our mouths." And then Jesus immediately responds with those gentle words: "Do not be anxious about your life... consider the lilies of the field... your Father knows your needs." (Matthew 6)

If your closets and drawers and storage areas are bulging, making you feel like you have no space in your life for new pursuits, no time in your life for new Adventures, please look at why you feel the need to accumulate rather than toss or donate the items you are not using. Where is there a lack of trust? Why is your security found in your stuff instead of God?

Accumulation shackles us in another way, as well. The bigger purchases we make enslave us to a certain level of income to sustain them. Often that "needed" income keeps us from pursuing the Adventure where God is calling because the Adventure would require a temporary, or even permanent, decrease in pay.

We can't go backwards.

Or can we? Do you have the courage to think this idea through? All kinds of fears and insecurities surface when we contemplate making big changes in our lives around the issues of money. *What will people think? Will they feel sorry for me and assume I'm a failure? How will my kids handle it if they don't have the things they're accustomed to having? Can I be happy without these things? Will I be OK?* If your Adventure is one that necessitates lowering your income to pursue, you need to find a way.

too much noise

One more area where fear keeps you shackled, besides your calendar and your stuff, is in your head. Simply put, your mind is too jammed to live a healthy and joyful life of Impactivity. Productivity, yes. Impactivity? You don't have the mental capacity to slow down and analyze why that's not happening. Perhaps this busyness is in the very area of your Dream. You've identified your Adventure and can honestly say that you're pursuing it, you're working hard at it. Very hard. Yes, very, *very* hard. Can't stop. Must. Keep. Going. Everything will fall apart if you slow down. The whole enterprise will crash. People will see that you're a failure. All your time and effort, wasted. The money you've spent or the money you thought you'd earn, gone. How will you pay the bills? Hold your head up?

If that description fits you in any way, I hope the spiritual issue at work here is already clear to you. Fear of being in need, fear of other people's opinions. Not trusting God to supply your true needs when you are living in obedience to your Adventure. Building your identity out of what others think. You can probably think of more fears if you take a bit of time right now to push down that path of thought. Can you go there? Get humble enough to admit that the very productivity on which you pride yourself is keeping you shackled and preventing your obedience. We often call ourselves "driven." We are proud of our energy, our commitment, our drive.

Please ask yourself, "what is driving me?" What is the force behind your frantic activity and refusal to balance your work with rest? What compels you to neglect relationships and your health? What is driving you away from a life of Impactivity?

simplify: practical steps to freedom

Hopefully you've taken some time to pause through the preceding section and think through, perhaps write down, the spiritual root of your cluttered day, house, and mind. And you've come to a place of repentance over the lack of trust that your fears represent.

You know it's time to change.

But change is hard.

Below I've outlined some practical, simple steps that will start you along the road to change. This isn't an overnight solution—and it's certainly not a panacea for the fear, clutter, and busyness that you face—but it's a step in the right direction.

find your identity

I wish there were a checklist or a simple how-to for switching off the tendency to define ourselves by the way we believe others see us. This tendency is so pervasive and so far-reaching that it is probably the single most important concept I can share with you. Until you release yourself from the hold of others, you will continue to make their opinions your purpose.

So get this identity question settled in your mind. Fully settled. Do more reading on God's unconditional love if you need to. Seek out Scripture that tells you the truth. Perhaps even talk it over with some of the people whose good opinions you are living for, and ask them to release you.

And then allow God to shape your steps as you walk toward your Adventure.

saying no

I'm probably not the first person to tell you this, but let me say it again: you must start saying No.

The clarity to see that your identity-building has led you to get over-involved with OPA will quickly lead you to a desire to cut the ties with the activities and busyness that are preventing your joyful Adventure. In a perfect world, you would approach those other people, explain your need to step away, and they would happily release you to pursue your dream. Of course, it doesn't always happen this way, and the fear of how it *might* happen can often paralyze you at this critical step of getting unshackled. After all, you say, it was my own insecurity that led me to say yes to OPA. Why should others suffer from my backing out? Perhaps I should just grit my teeth and power through, even though I now see that I am in the wrong place.

Well, perhaps you should. There is no right answer here. If the length of the commitment and the work still to be done are not excessive, you may decide that the responsible and loving thing to do is to stay the course. (Though I would still encourage you to search for someone who would joyfully replace you if possible.) But if the activity that is tying you up is not part of your Adventure and has a long and busy road ahead, you must get out. It is a simple as that. I know it is easy for me to say. Hard for you to do. I empathize with the hard task, the uncomfortable conversation you are facing. But you must do it. If you do not, you are the wicked and lazy servant in Jesus's parable who buried the gift given to him to invest, all because of fear. The kingdom of God is being built by people who form one body, working in harmony with each other in a beautifully complex orchestration. This harmony means that by obediently and joyfully living out your own Adventure, you will automatically participate in and assist the Adventure of others. But this orchestration does not happen if you are not playing your part, or if you are playing the wrong part. Your obedience is exactly what others need most.

I'll say it again: You must also start saying No, not only to indiscriminately filling the *needs* of OPA, but also to filling every *want* of those people in close relationship to you. Our wants expand to fill the willingness of others to supply them. It is human nature. Your spouse, your children, your friends, your boss will all desire for you to give them what they want, and the more you give, the more they will want. You cannot resent them for this (you are exactly the same!), but you must be on guard against it, and recognize when your want-filling is actually enabling their selfishness to grow.

breaking free of clutter

After all this saying No to others, it is time to start saying No to yourself. The clutter you are gripping must be released if you want to clear space for your Adventure and live in joyful Impactivity.

There are so many useful books, tools, and advice out there on decluttering. My problem with most of this advice is that it doesn't address the spiritual and emotional roots of how our clutter developed in the first place. We've all seen those reality TV shows about hoarders who are given a fresh new start with an organized home. You can barely keep a dry eye at the end of those shows, seeing the freedom that has been given to the person, the hope that this gift will change their lives forever. But most of us are aware of the true reality behind the TV show: they will likely go back to their hoarding ways. The deep insecurities and fears that have tied them to their clutter have not been broken, and therefore their homes and lives will fill up again with the useless weight of shackling clutter.

To truly break free from the shackle of clutter, you must do some spiritual decluttering before you do physical decluttering.

I don't mean to imply that it's a once-and-done effort. Releasing our hold on our own security is a huge step of growth and requires ongoing re-releasing. But understanding your need to trust God's provision should help you make your rounds through your home on a regular basis, purging away the clutter that is crowding out the mental freedom for creativity and dreaming.

Clutter-purging can seem overwhelming if you haven't been doing it regularly. You have drawers and closets, a garage and a basement, and even shelves and walls full of it. As I said, there is much practical advice to be found. Here is a quick and simple test to apply to everything: If you do not either *use* an item regularly or *love* the item because of its beauty or significance, get rid of it. It's not serving you in any way. Get rid of it. (*Fear creeping in? See previous section and escape!*)

Getting rid of things may seem like a simple trip to a homeless shelter or the Salvation Army, but it's so much more.

It's an escape from a shackle that's holding you back from your Adventure.

learning to trust

And while we're tackling fears, were you brave enough to think through the budgetary and income constraints that are keeping you shackled? Oftentimes one of the biggest barriers to Impactivity is the fear of lack of provision. We worry that if we pursue our Dream, we will lose income (even temporarily) and won't be able to provide for our families. And in doing so, will

79

fail the ones we love in a major way.

While the practical side of working out how to rid yourself of those big income commitments is very personal, I can give you some thought-starters that will help you get going. Obviously, if you are married, you're going to have to reach a place of agreement with your spouse first, and then together you can work through income decisions in a way that is honest, open, and that trusts God to provide even when the number at the bottom of the spreadsheet is red instead of black. This may take time and lots of conversation about your individual and shared Adventures and the need to be pursuing them.

To get you started, here's a list of income commitments to think through:

1. Your budget. Hopefully you have one! If not, this is the very first step to decreasing your income needs to enable you to pursue an Adventure that may lower your income. But assuming your budget is in place, comb through it for places to reduce. Don't be afraid to say No to some people's wants!

2. Your cars. If you have a car loan, consider selling the car to pay off the debt and then buying a less-expensive car with cash. This is a change that can be done relatively quickly. Analyze your feelings about other people's opinions and get your ego out of the way. Besides, living your Adventure will inspire them far more than the car you drive impresses them.

3. Your house. If you have a mortgage, your house is no doubt taking the biggest chunk of your income, including taxes, interest, and upkeep. Would you consider downsizing to a mortgage that perhaps has the same amount invested into principal but less into those other costs? What about the idea (radical thought alert) of selling the house and renting for a

while, still putting your principal amount into an investment, but saving yourself the interest, taxes, and repairs? I am not a financial consultant. This idea may not yield you the same equity in the long run. I am asking you to consider the possibilities.

4. Everyday expenses. Take a close look at the bills: cable and internet, cell phones, entertainment, groceries, eating out, gasoline, clothing, and all the rest. I would guess that you could skim a bit off every single category. Commit to eating out less? Buy some foods in bulk or reduce your trips to the store that result in impulse buying? Shop in consignment stores? Cut back on premium channels? You might be surprised at how small changes in many areas can reduce your "needs."

5. Interest on debt. If you can free up cash and you have consumer debt with high interest rates, focus on paying off that debt. When it's gone, you'll have freed up the extra cash you were using to pay it down, plus the payment you were already making on it.

escaping exhaustion

Whew. That was some hard stuff already. But there is more work to do. You may be pursuing your dream, but in a way that leaves you empty, exhausted, and burned out. You avoid OPA because you have a clear picture of your own Adventure, but living it out is making you frantic and overly busy. But we haven't yet discussed the spiritual root of this issue: your drive to achieve in order to feel valuable and worthwhile.

Drive is a good thing.

But the motive behind it may not be.

The advice in this section may seem far less practical than in the others. It may seem uninspired or unhelpful.

But, it's my real, honest advice. The upside is that it's fast.

Are you ready for it?

You just stop.

You embrace the idea of Impactivity—wholehearted and healthy living that will make a much bigger impact on the world than your frantic, exhausted, and overworked efforts ever could. You trust that the results of your scaled-back, slowed-down efforts will be as great as God wants them to be, and that anything more was only about you and your ego anyway.

Yes, you just stop.

Stop the spinning. Stop the rushing. Stop.

I will admit that for purposeful and often driven people like us, the idea of slowing down and getting less done is antithetical to everything we stand for. We tend to define success by only visible, tangible results and not the unseen, deeper impact we could have. To our way of thinking, pulling back means to become less successful.

I understand. Tying your self-worth to your success in the eyes of others or to your income makes you feel worthless if you don't see these results. Discouragement follows because all your efforts are "for nothing" (translation: have not gained you the success/money you desire). A resentment of wasted time and a questioning of your entire existence follows. Why are you doing all this if it's not going to be successful and/or earn good money?

The answer to those questions lies in your motivations.

You just stop because as long as success and money are your reasons, you will either be 1) crushed by your failure or 2) satisfied with an empty life if you succeed.

You just stop, because when you are spinning, you aren't seeing the greater *Why*—one that takes you through failure and reassures you that your efforts are worthwhile even if they gain you no recognition or payment.

You just stop because by embracing your Dream, you allow yourself to live joyfully and without regret you release tactics that aren't serving your *Why* to move on to better tactics that will better serve.

Understanding your *Why* is where you connect your Adventure to the needs of the world. It's a critical part of unshackling from all the lesser reasons we hold on to the tasks, clutter, and lifestyle that are keeping us from our Adventure. And we'll talk more about your *Why* in just a little bit.

journal

_____

_____

_____

_____

_____

_____

_____

_____

_____

_____

_____

_____

_____

_____

8

week two: the unshackling

The atmosphere in the Java Bean Cafe had gone from cozy to uncomfortable. Julia stared at the table, but she could feel the tension from the other women as well.

Last week's meeting had been fun, with all the talk of dreams and adventures. Julia had gone home and worked through Victoria's questions further, reminiscing backward to all the reasons she had started the cafe in the first place, remembering her initial excitement when she first opened its doors. She had even expanded that initial vision during her thinking and times of prayer this week, seeing the deeper reasons and the deeper purpose behind it all. From the beginning she had longed to create a place she felt was critically needed in her community—a place where people could meet in a relaxed, warm, unhurried atmosphere and share their lives with each other. She had come to work each day this week with a renewed sense of mission and energy to make this place a success. If she was honest, a couple of days of that excitement was enough to start the nagging fear that passion wasn't enough, because she simply couldn't work any harder than she already was. And no matter how hard she worked, things seemed to get more and more complicated.

But she had stuffed that thought away and focused on the Dream this week.

But now... now Victoria was saying that she'd never make it.

She had simply looked her straight in the eyes with that compassionate look that was becoming so familiar and told her that she'd never be able to sustain her work pace long enough to see this dream through. And it was all because of fear. Fear of failure, of what others would think, of not being seen as a success.

That stung.

Victoria was the first to break the silence. "What are you thinking, Julia?"

She winced. She wasn't ready to admit what she was thinking.

The woman's voice was gentle, but there was steel underneath. "Are you seeing any truth in the idea that you are burning out for the wrong reasons?"

Julia cleared her throat and risked a look at the other women. She needn't have feared their condemnation, because they were all looking somewhere else, anywhere but at Victoria.

"Um, yes. I guess so. I mean... it would be really hard to see this place fail."

"And you alone are responsible for its success?"

"Yes. Well, and God, I suppose."

Victoria smiled her knowing smile and let the weight of Julia's weak response sink in.

"Ok, I know that God is ultimately in charge of my success or failure. But don't I have to work hard at my dream? Isn't pursuing the Adventure *supposed* to be hard work?"

"Of course."

Julia sighed. "I don't get it. How can I just 'stop' as you say? Stop putting in the long hours, stop thinking about ways to improve even when I'm not here, stop obsessing over finances and suppliers and advertising and recipes and..." She shrugged. "It's *not* just about the way others see me. I have to make money here. That's the hard reality."

Across the table, Melanie was nodding.

But Victoria's attention was on Julia alone. "Julia, you are asking a question that does not yet deserve an answer. You are asking, 'how will I make a profit at my business if I stop using my business to create my identity? How will I be profitable if I unchain my self-worth from my success or failure?" Victoria's blue eyes held Julia's own gaze. "Do you see why your question is premature?"

She sighed. "Because I have to get my heart right. Get the spiritual issues resolved before I can even start thinking about the business issues."

Victoria's smile spoke more than words.

"But—"

The older woman held up a hand. "There will be time for asking questions about profitability. Your first task is to get free." Her glance shifted to the other women. "Melanie, I sense that you are feeling a bit shackled yourself. Did you have a chance this week to work on identifying your dream?"

Melanie fiddled with the large ring on her right hand. "I did, but I'm with Julia. It seems impossible, because of the money issue."

"Your dream is expensive?"

"No, not the dream itself. It might take a little money up front, but not much. No, it's the time it would take. I could never do it while keeping my job at the podiatrist's office."

Victoria nodded. "Adventures are time-consuming. It's part of what makes them so adventurous."

Julia felt a little pity at Melanie's expression. Victoria did tend to say things that sounded more like Gandalf than a real person.

"Melanie, let's assume that you are right. That there is no way you could do both—keep your job and pursue your Adventure. What would it look like to give up your job?

"Irresponsible."

"Hmm. Can you tell me why?"

"Yes. I've been thinking about it all week. I went home last Monday and really started dreaming about the acting troupe I'd like to direct, one that would perform in local venues to provoke thought and spark conversation about deeper issues I care about."

"Such as?"

"Literacy, for one. Poverty in our cities. Hunger." Melanie met Wanda's glance and gave her a little smile.

"Fascinating. So why would it be irresponsible? It sounds like you have a very caring, responsible heart."

"Because this acting troupe might make a little bit of

money to pay me for directing it, but the reality is that it's never going to pay as much as my office job. And I have two kids in college and another about to start. That job is paying for their education. "

"And what would your children do about college if you stopped?"

Melanie opened her mouth to answer, then closed it again. The silence lengthened.

Julia fidgeted, her leg bouncing a bit under the table, and felt the discomfort of everyone in the room. Well, everyone except Victoria.

"I... I guess they would have to get jobs to pay for it. Or maybe loans they'd have to pay off later. They could maybe go to less expensive schools..."

"In other words, they would have to take up the Adventure of their own lives, and stop letting you give up your Adventure for them?"

Melanie blew out a heavy breath and went back to studying the table. "Yikes. You don't pull punches, do you?" She rubbed her temples. "My husband won't understand all of this. He'll go crazy. I can just hear him—'Why should you get to do something so irresponsible as quitting your job to take up a silly hobby? What if everyone did that?'"

"Does he love you?"

Melanie nodded.

"Does he want God's best for you?"

Another nod.

"Then you must work *together* with your husband to figure out how you can both fulfill your true responsibilities and have income for your true needs, with nothing more than those needs, if money is keeping either of you from obedience."

Melanie blinked twice, at a seeming loss for how she could work *with* Todd.

"You are partnering together in life, Melanie. That partnership should include both of your Adventures. Begin with talking to him about his Adventure, about his dreams for his life. Has he reached them? Then I should think he would want the same for you. Has he not achieved his dream? Then I should think you can find ways for both of you to take this journey."

Julia glanced at Wanda and Gabrielle, who had been silent through all of this conversation. Perhaps they sensed that their turn was coming. From everything Wanda had shared, it was clear that she was running herself ragged like Julia. And Gabrielle was probably also afraid to step out and take a risk.

Victoria sighed. "You have one life, Melanie. You must determine whether you are called to work a job you dislike to save your children the inconvenience of assuming financial responsibility. It is one thing if you have the resources available and want to give them that gift. It is quite another to sacrifice your calling for it."

"I thought that's what mothers are supposed to do—sacrifice."

"We *do* sacrifice. We sacrifice our leisure time, our indulgences, our freedom to come and go as we please, sometimes our physical comfort, often our emotional comfort, and always our desire to be appreciated. We do not sacrifice our calling."

Melanie was close to tears, and Julia wished she could make all this stop, and yet It was good for Victoria to peel away their insecurities and fears to reveal where they were not acting in obedience to what God had for their lives.

"Melanie, you must take your Dream, your Adventure, to God. You must lay it down before Him, in all willingness to sacrifice it, if that is what He asks of you. But then you must listen very carefully to see what He says. He does not put both the calling and the refusal in your heart. You must discern which is from Him."

She took in the whole table of them with her glance. "All this talk of money is difficult, I know. There are many people who are barely making ends meet, who are working jobs they dislike to pay for food and diapers. They cannot simply walk away. The answers are not easy. The important thing is to *begin*. To recognize the choices that have forced your hand, to figure out the steps needed to create a solution, and to start taking those steps, however small."

They were still silent, and she gave them a compassionate smile. "Money comes and goes, ladies. It ebbs and flows. You can be content with little as easily as you can be content with much. But the Adventure! The chance to be part of the kingdom-building work of God! That is a pearl of great price, worth selling all you have to pursue."

Seeing their discomfort, she added, "Maybe it's time to relax for a while. More pastry?"

unshackle summary

escape

- Recognize where you are building your identity around others' opinions of you
- Identify areas you are in bondage to purchasing and accumulating
- Understand the spiritual issue at the heart of your over-productivity

simplify

- Discern the activities that are not part of your Adventure and pull back
- Clear out the clutter and make the hard changes to unshackle from purchases
- Make the decision to stop your frantic work pace and learn a better way

9

design
get ready

Let the favor of the Lord our God be upon us,
and establish the work of our hands upon us;
yes, establish the work of our hands!
Psalm 90:17

I n one sense, we've done the hardest work already. It's
tough to figure out the next Adventure of your life, and
then get free of everything that is preventing you from pursuing
it. If you've done the work (and not just read the book!), then I
am proud of you, and excited for you!

Now it's time to start designing what life in the Adventure
is going to look like. What does it look like to wake up every
day and work toward the dream? How will you get it all done?

How will you make money, if that's a part of your Adventure?

For years I grasped at every idea and opportunity presented to me. I didn't really understand myself and hadn't listened to myself or God enough to have a clear idea of where I wanted to go or how to get there. Then even as the destination began to get clear and I set some specific goals, I found myself with endless lists of to-dos. Some of these to-do items were vague and ill-defined projects. Some of them were tasks so specific I could have done them in less time than it took me to write them down. Everything that involved my work and my dream was lumped together with everything else in my life—money, family, home, health, personal growth. Some items had hard deadlines with disastrous consequences, some were nothing more than passing ideas. All these items massed together to form a chaotic, noisy jumble that left me feeling frantic and unable to slow down.

sketch the vision

Before your Adventure can get underway in a healthy manner, you need some groundwork in place. You need a clear sketch of where it is that you're headed, and a foundation of basic principles on which to build. Getting prepared for the Adventure is necessary whether you are starting a business, developing an organization or team, pursuing creativity, or simply going farther in the job you already have.

In sketching out your Dream and thinking forward to what it will look like, we are going to develop ideas around three things: your Vision, Strategy, and Tactics.

94

vision

The vision for your Adventure is the *Why* we have talked about already. It connects the work you do with the deeper reason for doing it. Vision paints a picture of what you want to create, how you want it to feel, what you want it to accomplish in the world, how you want your work to be viewed. Perhaps you've already given your vision some thought, even calling it by other names, such a "goal."

Many people—probably most—have goals. But I am going to encourage you to avoid that term.

Here's why: Almost invariably when people talk about goals, they are referring to something time-related. In fact, the acronym "S.M.A.R.T." goals has come into fashion, with the letters representing *specific, measurable, achievable, relevant,* and *time-bound.* There is nothing wrong with defining your goals. But in my opinion there is a problem with the necessity of goals and their associated time-bound deadlines *as a means to motivating action.*

Your vision should be so exciting, so inspirational, so perfectly aligned with who God has made you to be, that the last thing you need is a deadline. You are waking up most days ready to dive in. You can't wait to get started, and you have a hard time stopping. You don't need to motivate yourself with artificial timelines to create pressure as you work and feel guilt when you fail to meet them. If you need a deadline to motivate you, there may be something fundamentally wrong with your vision.

When we are driven by goals—by an arbitrary number and timeline—we are simply pursuing mediocre success. Only when we are driven by the joy that comes with knowing that we are following the Dream that God has for us, do we walk forward with a true desire to pursue our Adventure.

So what is your vision? It's a compilation of everything we've talked about thus far: all the uniqueness that makes up *you*, combined together with the needs you see in the world and the way in which you want to partner with God to love others. It's your Dream and the deeply-held reason you want to pursue it.

Take a few minutes and distill your vision down into a sentence or two. Don't worry about the wording being perfect or get stalled with the idea of a "Vision Statement." Get some thoughts down that make sense to you, something you can come back to later.

strategy

Goals can also get in the way of the second area, strategy. If the vision is the *Why* of what you do, then the strategy is the *What*. Strategy involves the specific ways in which you will go about accomplishing your vision. Having a plan is necessary, of course. But having too long-range of a plan (which is typical when we create goals) can limit us to only pursuing those things that were part of our plan and can cause blindness to bigger, better possibilities.

It is time to set your strategy for achieving your vision. What are all the ways you can see getting there? What are the types of work you would enjoy in pursuit of your dream? The areas in which you shine? The skills and abilities you can put to work? The opportunities you have through who you know, where you live, what you've already accomplished in your life? Resist the urge to look around to see what others are doing and copy their efforts. You are not those other people. What is joy for you will not be the same, and only work driven by joy will give you a life of Impactivity. Choosing strategies that work for others is a recipe for burnout, resentment, and failure. You must figure out what excites *you,* motivates *you,* feels like joy *to you.* Narrow all your ideas down to only those that meet these criteria.

The *Why* of your vision outlines the far-off destination of where you want to go. The vision will likely remain the same for as long as you are pursuing this Adventure. The *What* of your strategy tells you all the different types of transportation you'll take to get there. The strategies may grow and evolve over time, but they will be broad enough to carry you far and adaptable enough to change when the road changes.

So before you move on, have a list of perhaps three to five main strategies that will be your first projects.

It sounds like a lot of work, doesn't it? But interestingly, I think you will find yourself amazed at how much energy it will *create* as you begin to power your dream. Who needs deadlines? Who needs a done-by-this-date plan? Who needs that pressure when God is breathing life into the Dream that He created you for?

tactics

Once your vision and overall strategy are in place, it's time to get into tactics. If the strategy details the modes of transportation you'll take to reach the destination of your vision, then the tactics are the travel details. Tactics are the specific and logistical working out of your strategy. What route will you take? What kind of vehicle will it be? The analogy is

97

getting a little weak, but I hope you're getting the idea.

For example, if your vision is to run a fitness center because you deeply care about people being fit and healthy enough to live their full potential, and one of your strategies is to provide classes for the community, then your tactics can be all kinds of things—glow-in-the-dark Zumba®, rooftop yoga, I don't know! Go crazy! Unlike your long-range vision (the fitness center) and your medium-range strategies (holding classes), your tactics can vary widely and change often, as the need becomes obvious. Perhaps rooftop yoga seemed like a good idea, until people started complaining about the diesel fumes from the highway. Not a problem. Ditch the rooftop, and try basement yoga instead. (Ok, I realize I'm being ridiculous. If your Adventure really is to own a fitness center, I apologize.)

The point is that your tactics can involve your full creativity, without fear of failure, because they exist to serve your larger strategy, which will hold firm through the experimentation of various tactics. The strategy keeps you anchored. You're a rock climber with a harness, free to take some risks because the harness will keep your little slips from becoming disasters.

Having the anchor of a strategy also makes it less painful to switch tactics. You didn't fail. You experimented, learned, and adjusted to do something more effective. This freedom makes thinking up new tactics fun! So go ahead and brainstorm for as long as you can. It's not a To-Do List, so don't feel pressured if it gets long. It's an Idea List only at this point. We'll talk later about how to choose what to do first.

Far from being a dry exercise in travel-planning, the

brainstorming of tactics is a free-for-all. It's time to get crazy! Later you will start filtering this list into the best and brightest of your ideas. For now, generate as many as you can, and be as creative as you're able. Gather ideas from everything you read, hear, see. Read widely, pay attention, and put your skills and interests together in surprising and unusual ways. Go back to your handful of strategies and proceed through them one-by-one, asking yourself with each, "what are all the specific ways I can do this?"

create your manifesto

Once all this work on vision, strategy and tactics is done, I hope you will have pages and pages of scribbled notes, lists, and ideas. Is it a mess? Good! That means you've been creative.

But the free-roaming nature of our creative minds is not always conducive to the memory-retaining nature of our logical minds. So as fun as it was to map out your vision in a free and creative way, now it's time to get all of this designing into a coherent form we can refer to for guidance and inspiration.

I would encourage you at this point to create your own Manifesto. It sounds cheesy, I know. But it's powerful.

A manifesto is a declaration of all you believe and all you will be about in this exciting new pursuit of your Adventure. It is the distillation of your vision into a complete statement of your dream and the deeper purpose behind it, perhaps along with one or two of the main strategies you plan to employ to bring this dream to pass. There is no need to include tactics in your manifesto, since they may change before you finish writing. This document will be one that you can read every month, to bring you back to what you have decided in this moment is important enough to document. The manifesto is alive, and can grow and change as your Adventure unrolls before you. But there is a power in writing down the vision and how you plan to get there, and then taking some time before God to commit the entire sketch to Him.

prepare your initial tactics

Now that we have our manifesto done, it's time to do some more foundational work. You have this crazy list of tactics now, all kinds of ideas that might be possibilities. Some of them came to you as moments of genius, strikes of lightning. Some of them are just *meh*. It's time to apply some strategic 80/20 thinking to these tactics.

curate

A museum curator selects the best pieces for display, leaving others in the storeroom. You need to be the curator for your ideas. You're probably familiar with the 80/20 principle: the idea that 80% of your results will come from only 20% of the efforts you undertake. Before you jump into this list of tactics and start taking them one-by-one, either in the order they occurred to you or some other arbitrary order, let's narrow them down.

If you were to take your best guess, with all the information currently available to you, which of these ideas seems to be part of the 20% of the tactics that will give you 80% of the results you seek? (We call these the "vital few.") Which of them are probably part of the 80% of so-so ideas that might only move the needle another 20%? (We call these the "trivial many.") Just for fun, do the math on this one. Count all of the ideas on your big list of tactics and divide the count by five. That's how many total ideas you get to put on your 20% best-ideas list. So which ones will you choose?

I can hear you saying, "Whaaat? You just knocked out 80% of my great ideas!" Did I? Did some really great ideas get cut? Well, then, the even-better ideas on the 20% list must be *outstanding*! I can't wait to see what you accomplish with such amazing ideas! Can you accomplish every single idea on both lists? I doubt it. So why not begin with those you've identified as the absolute best, and leave the less-than-amazing ideas for later (or never)?

control your email

We have a few more preparations to make, to get organized, before we get to Ignite. Let's talk about email. If you are setting out to pursue any kind of Adventure that will involve other people, either as co-adventurers, employees, vendors, experts, or any other manner of human interaction, you are going to need to become an email ninja. If you do not, email will derail your day, stress your brain, dilute your clarity and generally make you crazy. Email is deadly.

The most toxic part of email is that it is a crazy mix of things to read, things to do, things to *think about* doing, and things to save. Because we get quickly overwhelmed by all the varying natures of this stuff coming at us, we avoid dealing with it. We let it pile up. Imagine that right before you were ready to leave for an appointment, someone handed you a box crammed with items taken from every room in your house, plus a few borrowed items that needed returning, along with your child's Christmas list when Christmas isn't for another six months, and the book your book club is reading together next. What would you do with that box? I know what I would do—shove it in a closet to deal with some other time. Now imagine that you were handed one of those boxes two, three, ten times a day. This is the crazy-making that is email.

It may seem like melodrama, but if you are going to live a life of Impactivity, you must take control of your Inbox. You must create a Trusted System outside of email (more on that system in a moment), and then you must diligently use this system to translate emails into tasks that need doing. Anything else represented by email should be trashed or filed. It's as simple as that. Do not use your Inbox as a combination filing cabinet/to-do list/reading list/photo album.

I'll talk more about alternative systems in a minute, but before I do, I highly recommend the process commonly referred to as "Inbox Zero" as a methodology to keep email under control. It has really helped me to tame my inbox and to keep me on track toward my Adventure.

trust your system

Now, more on that Trusted System. Just like email, if you're living wholeheartedly in your Adventure and always jotting down ideas, your tasks might quickly overwhelm you. So many ideas! So many things going on at once, both professional and personal, creative and mundane. Appointments, meetings, and phone calls. Urgent deadlines and important projects with no deadlines at all. It can be a real mess. Remember, mental clutter prevents Impactivity. It causes disorganization and therefore stress, and it impedes creativity. One of the most important things you can do is to set up a Trusted System where you can organize your life. There are so many ways to do this, and if you'd like more specific guidance, I'd suggest *Design*, as mentioned above. But here are some general guidelines:

1. Your system should have a way to have tasks disappear into it until you need to see them. You don't want to have to look at a to-do item before you are able to actually take action on it. The old-school executives back in the day called this a "tickler" file system. You can still use this system if you're a low-tech kind of person. A tickler file consists of forty-three folders: one for each day of the month (1-31) and one for each month of the year (Jan-Dec). Your thirty-one daily folders all get put behind the current month's folder, and then the rest of the months go behind that. Whenever you want to postpone seeing something or taking action on it, you put it into the day (or month) in the future when you want to see it. Every day you look in today's folder (e.g., August 17th) for anything that needs doing and rotate that folder to the back. On the first day of the next month, you take out anything in that month's folder and distribute it through the daily folders.

I'm guessing you're going to want something digital. There are amazing apps out there, many of them free, that can accomplish this same feat, with the added benefit of adding visible and audible reminders to make sure you don't miss a thing. Even something as general as Google Calendar can give you this ability to schedule future—and even recurring—tasks. We don't have space in this book to outline all the details of setting up your system, but if you need more specifics, please see the workbook *Design: How to Create a Vision and System for your Life.* Take some time to set up all your deadline-oriented tasks, appointments, and meetings in your system. Put everything in there that you currently hold in your brain (successfully or not!).

One important thing: Do not create fake deadlines for tasks that do not actually have deadlines, no matter how important those tasks are to you. Fake deadlines are like mini-goals, and they are counter-productive. They make you feel stress and pressure unnecessarily. Work from joy. If you need fake deadlines, figure out why you're not joyful about that task and rectify it somehow.

2. Your system should allow you to file ideas into folders, whether literal or digital. You will have folders for the projects, with tasks and ideas inside related to your Adventure and to the rest of your life. It's a great idea to divide these folders into your 80/20 lists, so you know where to go for your best stuff.

3. Your system should allow you to set priorities. It is very helpful to see at a glance (through color coding or some other method) which projects and tasks are the most important to you, especially those projects and tasks that don't have deadlines.

Again, this has been the briefest of overviews in setting up a Trusted System, and there is much more practical advice in *Design*.

■

You are ready to Ignite! Your blueprint sketch of vision, strategy and tactics has been drawn. You've done the foundational preparation of getting a system in place that keeps track of your 20% of best ideas, your true deadlines, and your priority projects and tasks.

I would add only one more thing to this phase of preparation. Accountability. You are about to embark on something amazing. You will face roadblocks and obstacles— from within and from without—that will test your ability to remain focused, your commitment to the Adventure, your freedom from striving for the good opinions of others, and freedom from the many fears that can derail you. One of the best things you can do is share your commitment to Impactivity with one or more trusted friends who will understand and keep you coming back to the Dream, to the Unshackling, and to your Design. This may be a local friend or an online friend, a professional group like a Mastermind Group, or a collection of friends all trying to live a life of Impactivity. Share your heart with them, then let them protect, challenge, and encourage you while you do the same for them.

You can also join the amazing community of like-minded people at impactivity.com.

journal

10

week three: the designing

W anda had her eyes on Melanie the whole time Victoria was telling them about the Design component of Impactivity. Melanie was writing notes as fast as she could, and was practically glowing with excitement. When Victoria finished, Wanda had to ask.

"You seem like you're on fire tonight, Melanie. After last week, you seemed so discouraged about following your dream."

Melanie grinned and nodded. "You wouldn't believe what happened this week. I talked with my husband about all of this, and he understood! No, more than understood, he agreed with me. He even wanted to think through some of this Impactivity stuff to apply to himself. We started figuring out how we could make it all work. The next day I talked to the podiatrist I work for, and he agreed to let me cut back to part-time. Todd and I will make some cuts in the budget, including letting our kids know they'll need to work a bit harder for tuition," at this she glanced at Victoria triumphantly, "and so we shouldn't really feel the loss of income too much. With the extra time I'll have, I'm going to start the acting company!"

"Awesome!" Gabrielle slapped the table, making them all jump and then laugh.

"Isn't it?" Melanie pointed to her notebook. "That's why I'm writing all this down so fast tonight. Though I have to admit, I'm still a little confused about the difference between vision, strategy, and tactics."

Wanda nodded. She had been thinking the same thing. "Yeah, I'm getting a better picture of my dream, too. And this week I started figuring out what's holding me back. But I'm still not sure where to start."

Victoria sipped her usual lemon-water. "I think we'd all love to hear more about the Dream and the Unshackling first, Wanda."

There were nods all around.

She took a deep breath. "OK, this might take a while to explain. I told you about the food distribution thing in the alley behind the restaurant. And you know I've been wanting to get out of the restaurant business. I always figured that one day I'd go back to catering to make money, but I also knew I wouldn't be ready to sell the restaurant and earn less for years yet. And to be honest, catering isn't really my dream at this point in my life either. So I got to thinking this week about my real dream, and all the things that are holding me back. And I realized that my husband and I have been talking about downsizing for years, since the kids left home. If we sold the house and moved into the vacant apartment over our restaurant, we'd have a good nest egg earning dividends from the sale of the house. I could afford to hire someone to run the restaurant if he also resurrected the catering business to bring in extra earnings. I think I could work myself out of the day-to-day operations pretty quickly."

"Fabulous!" Victoria clapped her hands. "And then what?"

"And then I've already started working on what comes next." She hesitated.

They all waited, knowing how difficult it was to feel exposed.

The words came out in an embarrassed rush. "I'm going to start a program teaching cooking and catering skills to women who are living in shelters." She was even more embarrassed when Melanie practically squealed and reached across to hug her.

"That is fantastic, Wanda." Julia was grinning too.

Gabrielle was nodding, eyes shining.

She shrugged. "I figure I can even maybe hire some of them to help with the restaurant's catering, if I find some with the aptitude."

"Bravo, Wanda!" Victoria beamed at her.

"But it's a long road ahead to make all this happen. And that's why I'm getting a little confused about all this strategizing you're talking about."

"Of course." Victoria nodded. "Let's make it practical." She inclined her head toward Melanie. "You've told us your dream of starting this acting troupe that will perform in ways that will spur conversation about important issues. That is your vision. What are the ways your acting troupe will get that done?"

Melanie looked into the distance, thinking. "Well, there are a few main ways, I guess. We'll do full-length plays that will be performed at the community playhouse. And I'm thinking shorter pieces that we could perform in high schools or churches or even coffeehouses."

"Maybe even here?" Julia asked.

Melanie smiled. "I hadn't even thought of this place. I guess we'll have to talk! I'd also like every member to be involved in some cause in the community, so that we're doing more than just performing about what we believe in." She brought her attention back to Victoria. "Is that what you're talking about?"

"Yes, exactly. Those are your main strategies. You will likely develop a few more as you move forward. Now, what are your tactics? What are the specifics of how you will get all that done?"

"Oh, I won't bore you with all that. Trust me, I've already got a mile-long list, starting with recruiting and then finding writers, contacting the playhouse. The list goes on."

"Good. And also realize that all your ideas for specific performances and locations, everything from the topics you'll address to the costumes you'll wear, they're all part of your tactics. Tactics are the place where almost all your ideas live. The benefit to understanding the middle layer of strategy is that you will always be coming back to your few strategies, to help ensure your tactics are in line and not getting too scattered or random or ineffective. And your strategy in turn will always be checked against the vision, to ensure everything is staying the course."

Melanie was nodding and writing furiously.

Wanda felt the strange and surprising eagerness of a seven-year-old, wanting to raise her hand and jump up and down saying "Me next, me next!"

Victoria turned to Wanda. "Ok, Wanda, now let's talk about how your dream is going to come to life. What are the specific ways you're going to benefit women in shelters?"

"I just have the one idea—teaching cooking classes."

"Is that all they need to know? Why do you want them to learn to cook?"

"It's more than the cooking. I want to give them job skills they could take to a restaurant, or the ability to run their own little catering businesses. Something to help them get back on their feet."

"It sounds like you have in mind a more organized *program* of courses, something that women could move through progressively. Maybe even offer some kind of certification that would mean something on a job application?"

"Yes, exactly." Wanda laughed. "Though I hadn't thought of that certification thing. It's a great idea."

"So you can see that there is a strategy here. You have a bigger vision than simple cooking lessons. You want to use cooking skills to empower women to make a better life for themselves. The cooking itself is only one part of that vision. You will have various strategies to make it happen."

"I'm getting it." She made a few notes.

"And the tactics?"

"I guess I could teach different culinary arts courses, like I learned in restaurant school. Meats and poultry. Pastas and sauces. That sort of thing. Maybe pastries."

Julia laughed. "I hate to make everything about me, but hey, if my dream keeps developing like I hope, I'll soon be looking for someone to help here with pastries!"

They laughed at the coincidence, but Victoria wasn't laughing.

"Nothing happens by accident, my friends. There is a reason you are here together, experiencing the start of Impactivity together. Perhaps many reasons."

She let that hang in the air a moment, but then came back to Wanda. "Your different courses are tactics, yes. As are the different shelters where you may teach, the different ways you will make your program known to women in need. Many tactics will be necessary to get this dream moving and some will work better than others. You will keep coming back to the strategy of your program, and the vision of empowering women to make a better life, bringing every tactic in line with both of those and choosing the very best of them."

Wanda sighed. "It's a bit overwhelming."

"Yes, all the best dreams are. That's why you are going to create a Trusted System to handle all the details and then discipline yourself to keep everything in that system." Victoria looked to Gabrielle and Julia. "Don't think I have forgotten about the two of you. Let's talk more about how to strategize those dreams."

The meeting went long that night, but they each went away energized, ready to brainstorm and set up systems so they'd be ready to Ignite, which Victoria promised was going to be the most fun of all.

design summary

sketch

- Create a compelling vision that needs no goals
- Decide on strategies that will best accomplish your vision
- Brainstorm tactics to accomplish your strategies

prepare

- Curate your ideas to the vital 20%
- Use a method to keep email controlled
- Create a trusted system to organize your entire life

11

ignite
do the work

In all toil there is profit,
but mere talk tends only to poverty.
Proverbs 14:23

It's time to Ignite! All the dreaming, the getting free, the
planning and getting prepared, they've all led up to this
moment, when the work truly begins. Ready? Go!

What's that? You're not sure what to do first? Which
project to choose? When to work on your Adventure and when
to do the rest of life? I get it.

One of the areas where I struggle the most is the constant
arranging and rearranging of the tasks I want to accomplish. I
can think of a hundred ways to sort them, and so many fun

ways to organize them (color-coded spreadsheet, anyone?). This analysis feels like anything but Igniting. More like smoldering, or maybe even sputtering out. Sometimes this hesitation is about fear, as we have touched on earlier. But often it is simply part of my personality, as a driven person who sees every single task as a priority and gets stuck figuring out which priority to do first.

You may be similar, or perhaps you shun all that organization, but simply feel lost as to where to start.

Beyond your overarching strategy, you need a daily workflow that will get you from point A to point B successfully, not neglecting all the healthy behaviors and responsible actions you need to take to be truly living in Impactivity. Because your Adventure is so exciting, with all its associated strategies and tactics, you may be tempted to go head down, barreling through, and end up right back on the productivity treadmill, in which you are burning out and getting unhealthy. And that's exactly what we are trying to escape.

We're going to talk about four ways you can make the most of each day, building Impactivity into your life while still attending to everything you must.

habitize

No, habitize is not an actual word. But I'm using it anyway, to help you understand the intentionality that habits should involve. You are going to *habitize* your life.

Habits are your new secret weapon in your life of Impactivity.

If you've ever taken determined steps to get yourself

healthy in every area of life and made a list of all the things you should do in a day to get there, you've probably felt the frustration of the length of that list, and the annoying fear that you won't have time for anything else. Just managing all those healthy actions feels like a chore and *doing* them seems like it will take all day.

Enter habits.

A bit of time spent on intentionally setting up good habits will reap great rewards into the future. The major reason why habits are so powerful, whether good or bad, is that they bypass the moment of choice. When an action is habitual, you don't think. You don't consider. You don't choose. You simply act.

If you've never given thought to habits, other than to notice when a good habit or bad habit naturally forms in your life, then you may not have noticed that habits have three distinct parts to them: the event, emotion, or circumstance that starts the habit (sometimes called the "cue" or the "trigger"), the behavior of the habit itself, and the reward (healthy or unhealthy) that performance of the habit brings. By analyzing these three components and manipulating them to your advantage, you can intentionally construct habits you wish to implement in your life. With all the details of your Adventure, plus the rest of your life that must be managed, the more actions you can offload into the automatic action of habits, the easier your day will run.

Think through every single thing you'd like to do consistently. Run through all the areas in which you're striving for health: physical, spiritual, emotional, mental, relational. Every one of those areas probably has supporting actions you'd like to perform daily. You can probably come up with a lengthy list. Once you have this list, dissect those habits and figure out how to create something to trigger each one, and an associated healthy reward that can help pull you through the behavior. This reward should be something more immediate and tangible than the long-term benefit the habit will also bring.

For example, if you are trying to eat healthier, the long-term benefits to your body are obvious. But that far-off reward isn't always enough to motivate action, is it? Can you construct a more immediate reward? Maybe you "earn" your morning coffee only when you eat protein for breakfast. Obviously, you are the only one monitoring your actions and rewards here, but a little planning ahead and some structure can go a long way in helping with motivation.

Set reminders on your phone, place notes around your house—do whatever you need to do—to create these triggers. When the idea of the habit enters your consciousness via the trigger, it's your time to perform it. Do not give yourself the option of a choice.

Start small with your list. Too many new habits at once will likely discourage you. As they become more automatic, start stringing them together. That way performing a few them in quick succession turns into a single habit in your mind. For example, I have a single "Morning Routine" habit that is actually a chain of several habits linked together, including eating my protein breakfast, taking my vitamins, stretching, blitzing through email, and planning my day. If you want to dive deeper into creating habits, see *Habitize: A 7-Day Guide to Changing Your Life*.

Habits don't belong on your to-do list or your calendar. They don't get checked off. You can't make them up tomorrow if you don't do them today. They are the "given" part of your day that requires no thought. You will be amazed at how much it helps to simply clear out the need for *thinking* about many of these behaviors and deciding whether to do them now or later, today or tomorrow. Choice removed. Action taken. Move on to the exciting things.

prioritize

Next up after incorporating habits into your daily workflow is creating priorities. Most over-achievers are really challenged by the concept of prioritizing. All of it gets a red flag, a #1. But when everything is a priority, then nothing is a priority. Your first challenge is to do some sorting.

I would suggest that you first separate everything in your life—every task and project—into two categories: those that are part of your Adventure and those that are not. You are doing this for both clarity and scheduling purposes. Too often we can run through our day in reactive mode, responding to the most urgent needs, putting out fires, letting others (and email!) dictate our schedule. At the end of the day, you may feel productive, but have you made any progress on the things you have identified as your calling in life? By separating everything into these two categories, it becomes easier to see all the responsibilities that are outside of that calling, whether by necessity or choice. You may decide to pause here and take a run through unshackling again, if you find that your to-do list of tasks outside your Adventure is already enough to fill more than twenty-four hours in a day.

Once you have your list divided, it is time to divide your

119

day. Don't constantly shift back and forth between home and personal tasks, Adventure tasks and all the other stuff of life. Give yourself the gift of a set time of day, or a set day of the week, or whatever you can manage, to focus on your Adventure, and keep everything else outside that time. Or if your schedule varies, create a weekly habit of planning the week ahead. Only you can decide when the best time is, but I would suggest you give ample thought to what time of day is your most energetic, productive, and focused. For most people, it will be first thing in the morning. But if you are home with young children, it could be that afternoon nap time or after the kids are in bed is your only time to truly focus. Or if you are working a job that requires you to leave the house early, the late-night hours might be your best option. One caution: protect both this time and your energy during it. Do whatever it takes to keep it free so you can give it to your Adventure, and do whatever it takes to be energetic and ready to focus when it arrives.

But setting aside time to tackle your Adventure still doesn't help you to accomplish the difficult task of knowing which of your tactics to work on first. How do you prioritize your strategies so you know what to do first (and what to do last)?

The good news: Because of the work you've already done in your journey toward Impactivity, this task isn't going to be difficult. If you've had trouble prioritizing in the past, it was probably because you didn't have a clear vision. You hadn't identified the handful of strategies that would work best to accomplish the Dream. You either had no tactics, or you hadn't narrowed down your list of tactics to the absolute best 20% that would yield 80% of the results you wanted. But now you

120

have all those things sorted out, which makes prioritizing (dare I say it?) easy.

You can do this now!

If you have a short list of tactics that all seem equally valid and are not dependent on one another in a way that suggests a natural order, then just pick one and start! They're all good ideas. Just get moving. In other words, there is no formula to prioritizing correctly, no magic order that will guarantee results. You've done the work to narrow down your options. Now you can simply start on one of them.

And what about all the projects and tasks that aren't part of your Adventure, but must be accomplished anyway? Hopefully you have all these in your Trusted System, set up to remind you when they need to be done. If everything on this list is of a "do it now" nature, and the time needed to keep up with these tasks is always more than the available time you have, then you need to unshackle. Something needs to change. Of course, occasionally these tasks will pile up faster than the time you've allotted for them. Perhaps you've been sick or traveling, or there's been some unexpected and time-consuming circumstance that put everything on hold. When this happens, schedule a "catch-up day" for yourself and put everything but your habits on hold while you power through as many small tasks as possible. But again, if these catch-up days are happening too often, you probably need to reevaluate your scattered involvement in too many things.

By this time you should be starting to get a feel for what your daily workflow is going to look like. If you are a full-time entrepreneur or business owner, you may have the entire day to play with, to divide into large chunks of time devoted to pursuing your Adventure and the time you need to spend on everything else. But if you still (or always) will need to work another job, these chunks of time will look different for you as you divide up your available evening and weekend time. Whatever your schedule looks like, develop one that can be relatively consistent. This consistency becomes part of your habits as well: a start time and an end time for working, a consistent time for meals and the habits you've constructed.

focus on one project

Once you have your daily habits in place as a non-negotiable part of your day, you've protected the time necessary to work on your Adventure, then it's time to choose a strategy and get to work on the tactics that are part of that strategy. (And, yes, you must focus your decision to choose a single strategy. We all like to have multiple projects going at once, don't we?)

If you've put your ideas through the process of curating them down to the best 20% and you still have many different possible paths to take, develop the discipline now to start focusing your decisions. I say "now" because it is only going to get harder. The more successful you become as you pursue your Adventure, the more opportunities are going to open to you. This widening of your possibilities that comes with success is one of the reasons why I believe long-range goals are pointless. But there is also an inherent danger here. Imagine your journey as a single path on which you are making good progress. But at the first significant marker of your progress, the path suddenly branches into three paths, all of them with wonderful and different destinations you could not have predicted. Fantastic! You will get somewhere better than you had dreamed. But still, you can only choose one path. Attempting to walk down three paths at once just doesn't make sense, does it? And it will mean certain failure.

For example, imagine you have studied to become a computer programmer and are eager to start working on creating some amazing apps that will help people in important ways. You get a job designing websites for local businesses to pay the bills, while working on your Dream on the side. But it turns out you are very good at your bill-paying job, more clients begin seeking you out to design their sites and you get very busy. Before long, one of your clients wants you to come work for her alone, in a high-pressure job with long hours. If being a self-employed app-creator is still your Dream, then the widening of your opportunities here is not necessarily a good thing.

Now understand: every single day you are standing at the head of these multiple paths. Your life is a series of choices, and so is the pursuit of your Adventure. You must carefully evaluate every opportunity that comes to you, and not fall into the trap of thinking you must grab at each of them out of fear of missing something. Pursuing everything at once will undermine your progress in every area. Some opportunities may be terrific and hard to refuse, but if they don't help you pursue your Adventure, you must refuse them if you want to make progress on an even-better opportunity.

There is more to focusing than choosing opportunities, however. There is also the focusing of your *mind* on a single task at a time. Do not be fooled by the concept of multitasking. It is a fallacy. While it might be possible to focus your *attention* on one thing while your *body* performs an unconscious action, it is not possible to focus your conscious mind on more than one thing at once. We often believe we are accomplishing this impossible feat, but that belief comes from the ability to switch tasks very fast. Start calling this behavior *switch-tasking* rather than multi-tasking, and you'll become more aware of the wasted time, the lost concentration and the diluted creativity that it causes. You have put so much effort into narrowing down your Dream, your strategy, your tasks, and your day into this one block of time you are giving to your Adventure. Do not waste it by jumping around to check email, answer the phone or texts, chase rabbit trails online, run loads of laundry, or whatever else tempts you away from the work at hand.

Focus on the task at hand.

And trust that God is leading you towards something much bigger than the frantic pace you've been working at for so long.

multiply

If you have put everything we've covered thus far into practice, you are no doubt by now doing amazing things. With your newfound freedom from all that was dragging you down and habits in place to keep you healthy and balanced, you have a sense of well-being surrounding all of your life. With a clear direction to the Dream you want to pursue, scheduled blocks of time to work on it, and focused attention while you work, you are knocking tactics out left and right, and getting a good sense of where this Adventure is going to take you next. A taste of this kind of Impactivity is going to make you want more.

And more.

You're at a critical point here. It's at this point, when everything is going well, that you will likely face the temptation to slide back into unhealthy patterns. *If I just skipped my morning block of habits today, I could get more done on that fun project I started yesterday.* Or maybe, *the family will understand if I don't get the food shopping done tonight, since I've been so busy.* Your Adventure and all its joy is calling out to you, tempting you to overindulge.

I understand! But please do not go back to the shackled place again. Like the widening opportunities that come to you when you are successful but can dilute the focus that brought you success, greater Impactivity also brings the temptation to forsake Impactivity with a return to mere productivity. You must be on guard.

With that said, however, there are a few ways to multiply your needed resources of time, money and energy to get more done.

multiply your time

1) Find more time in your twenty-four hours by figuring out where you are most likely to waste time. If you find yourself switch-tasking, working on mindless activities you're using to "relax" but aren't really relaxing, working on OPA, getting stuck on the internet, doing the 80% of stuff that doesn't make much difference, take note of it and stop.

2) Guard your hours. Don't let your sudden influx of time tempt you to give it all away to others who would love to have it. (Remember, you are not refusing to serve people; you are focusing your service to the Adventure where you're called.)

3) Invest every minute. Figure out ways to automate as

much as possible in your life, and search out every part of your life that you can possibly delegate to others, whether for payment or by some other arrangement.

multiply your money

The Impactivity-driven reason to multiply your money is not to be able to buy more things. Buying more will only shackle you. We multiply money because it often takes money to fund the Adventure, or because giving it away is part of the Adventure. The process to multiply your money is much the same:

1) Find more money by figuring out where you're wasting it. Cut back on luxuries, develop a budget and stick to it, and spend strategically.

2) Guard your resources. Don't let your sudden influx of money tempt you to spend it on something unnecessary.

3) Invest well. Just like with your time, find ways use your money to pay for more delegation, or to cut back on your current job so you can pursue your Adventure.

multiply your energy

1) Find more energy by eating healthy food, getting good sleep, exercising your body, and learning how to truly rest. (Many of us mistake "true rest" for "leisure," a topic we will talk more about in Chapter 13, Recharge.

2) Guard your energy. Your energy will be attacked by a craving for super-productivity, by poor planning, by people draining you, by exhausting tasks from which you need to unshackle.

3) Invest your energy into what really matters. Rejuvenate,

truly rest, and then use that extra energy to focus your attention on the Adventure!

You have been through quite a process since you first began Dreaming. You now have everything in place to get amazing things accomplished. But for true Impactivity to change your life, you will need to take another step, past the work and into the rest. You will need to Recharge.

journal

_____

_____

_____

_____

_____

_____

_____

_____

_____

_____

_____

_____

12

week four: the igniting

T he Java Bean Cafe's signature jazz music was all that could be heard for several minutes, aside from the scratching of pens on paper and clicking on laptops. Melanie was trying to get it all down—Victoria's advice for Igniting, plus her own reactions to it and all the ideas it spurred. So many ideas!

She'd been super excited over the past week to get her Trusted System in place, all set up with her recurring tasks, appointments, and reminders. It was amazing how freed up she felt, knowing that everything was in one place, where she could trust the system to remind her of important things at the right time. And email! Ah, what a relief it had been to finally clear out that Inbox. She had appreciated Victoria's permission to simply move most of it to a "Processed Mail" folder and start fresh. True, it wasn't all "processed" in the legitimate sense, but she knew she wasn't ever going to look at it anyway, and she knew where to find it if she ever did need it. She'd been keeping on top of getting the Inbox emptied every day. Between the decluttering of her house, the simplifying of her calendar, the cutting back of work hours, and all the mental noise that had disappeared into her Trusted System, Melanie was feeling like she'd been given a whole new life. By Friday, her first day off from the podiatrist's office, she was *so ready* to get started on her new Adventure.

But all day Friday, she'd been a little lost. She was home for the day, so it made sense to keep the laundry going. And the boys were coming home from college for the weekend, so she should really get some food in the house. Plus, she'd been meaning to get started on exercising more regularly, so now that she had the time, that was clearly an important thing to do.

By lunchtime, frustrated with herself, she finally sat down at her computer, determined to make some progress. But where to start? Even though she had narrowed down her list of tactics and ideas to the top 20%, she still was unsure which of them to choose first. Then the washer buzzed, so she went to switch the loads and think about it. An hour later, she roused herself from an article she was reading online—a link a friend had sent in an email—and realized she had forgotten to choose which project to start with. And how did it get to be 4:00 already?

The weekend flew by, hanging out with the family, going to church. Should she have been working on her Adventure? She wasn't sure.

Today she was back to her office manager job, so by the time she'd reached the Java Bean tonight, she was more than ready for all of Victoria's advice on how to Ignite.

The rest of the women were slowing down in their note-taking, as she was, so she started the conversation. "I'm loving this."

Nods all around.

Gabrielle stretched, arms flexing, like she was getting ready to Ignite right then. "Me too! This step just puts it all together for me. After this past week, I've finally got a clear vision on my dream to start this wedding coordinator business, but it's going to be awhile before I can quit at the florist shop. She smiled at Melanie and Wanda. "I'll admit I'm a little envious of both of you, having the resources to make big changes right away—cutting back your hours at your job and in the restaurant."

Julia snorted a laugh. "Ah, just look at me, then, and you'll feel better. I'm working on this dream night and day."

"Sorry, Julia." She looked at her notes. "But seriously, I think I can make some good progress now with this plan. I don't have too much free time, but I can start dividing it into the two categories you talked about, Victoria. And making sure I'm getting time for both."

Victoria nodded. "I'm glad you see how even with a full-time job, there is room for an Adventure."

"Definitely! In the past, my evenings and weekends have been so random. But I can see now that they've been a combination of habits, wasted time, pursuing my dream a little bit, and all the rest of the life-stuff that needs doing. I haven't had a real plan." She glanced at her notes. "But this makes it feel doable."

Melanie pointed at Gabrielle. "Yeah. What she said."

Victoria laughed.

"But there's more," Melanie said. "Now that I'm on a roll, I feel like I can find even more time, money and energy in all the places I've been wasting it, and funnel all of it into the blocks of time where I'm focusing my complete attention on my Adventure."

Victoria nodded to Melanie. "And how will you decide which of your many ideas to work on first? You mentioned when we first arrived that Friday afternoon sort of disappeared in a cloud of indecision for you."

Melanie frowned. "I feel like you're saying that it doesn't matter what I choose first. Is that true?"

The older woman glanced at each of the others. "What do you all think?"

Wanda leaned forward, elbows on the table. "Yeah, I think that's what she's saying. We've gotten everything so narrowed down and focused now, with only our best ideas out there. So we just choose one and start moving. I think this has been my problem. Every time I've thought about my dream in the past, I didn't know where to start. And since I believed there was only one perfect place to start, I didn't start at all. Waiting for some kind of guarantee, like she said a few weeks ago."

Julia was nodding and smiling.

And, Melanie noticed, her leg was perfectly still.

Julia leaned forward. "I am so excited about this cafe now. More excited than I've been since I first opened the doors. Over the past two years I've thought of a million ways to make more money, to do more advertising, to expand the menu, to narrow the menu, longer hours, shorter hours—I've never been able to have a solid plan, and I've gotten so lost in the details.

I'm finally seeing that I need to start hiring, even though it means less profit, so I can be freed up to work on this business in a focused way that will generate more income."

After a moment of thoughtful silence, Melanie said what she guessed they were all thinking. "Impactivity is a long process, though, isn't it? It's going to take us awhile to work through all of this and really put it into place."

Victoria spread her hands to take in all of them. "But you have come so far already. Yes, it will take time. And there is actually much more to learn about each of these elements. I have given you just enough to get started, to see the need. And if you will continue to meet here on Mondays, I will pop in now and then to check on you and to give you more when you are ready."

"So you're finished with us for now?" Melanie frowned. "But I thought you said there were six elements to Impactivity."

"Ah, yes, my Adventurers. We are not finished yet. We still have two elements critical to Impactivity yet to cover. And the next may be your most favorite element yet. I will see you here next Monday!"

ignite summary

habitize

- Outline the everyday healthy habits in every area of life
- Create triggers and rewards for each habit
- Link habits together in "chains" to accomplish more

prioritize

- Split projects and tasks into categories
- Divide your day to protect time for your Dream
- Create workflows for Habits, Dream, and the rest of life

focus

- Focus your decisions to advance one project at a time
- Focus your attention a single project without multitasking

multiply

- Multiply your time by investing in automation and delegation
- Multiply your money by investing in hiring
- Multiply your energy by guarding your physical health

13

recharge
stop to rest

Unless the Lord builds the house, those who build it labor
in vain. Unless the Lord watches over the city, the
watchman stays awake in vain. It is in vain that you rise up
early and go late to rest, eating the bread of anxious toil;
for he gives to his beloved sleep.

Psalm 127:1-2

I want you to think about the difference between a single
flame and a roaring fire. A single flame, say a candle, burns
small and it burns slow. It has steady fuel. But it still makes a
huge difference in a dark room. A roaring fire, on the other
hand, devours all the fuel of the room quickly, and then burns

out, leaving nothing but ashes and giving no light.

I want your life to be the steady flame of a candle in the darkness, not a devouring fire that burns through your health, your relationships, and your energy, leaving you exhausted and ineffective. Burned out. This steadiness and longevity are the critical piece of a life of Impactivity. Without that steadiness, you can only be productive for a short time. We rest so that we can work more, yes, but for so many other reasons as well, including to enjoy all that God has given us, while we trust Him to keep our world spinning without us.

And as hard as it may be to slow down when we are doing something we love, the flame of our life can only burn steady and long if it is continually refueled. Recharged.

rest

Everyone is always saying they're too busy. Have you noticed that? It's rare to come upon a person, ask "how ya' doin'?" and get the answer, "I'm so bored. I have nothing to do." We fill up our time and attention easily, and somehow even when it feels like things aren't getting accomplished, we still feel *so busy*.

The truth is, most of us like being busy. We don't actually want to be idle, at least not forever. But there is also an exhaustion pulling at us that forces us to rest, sometimes grudgingly, sometimes with great relief because life has been wearying. And yet, even after our "down-time," we don't feel refreshed. Just postponed.

I would suggest to you that we don't want more rest. We want *better* rest. And we don't really want less busy. We want our busyness to have purpose. We have spent much of this book thus far talking about shifting from mere productivity (busyness) to Impactivity (productivity + lasting impact). Those are great things, but you will never have Impactivity if you don't have rest.

It sounds simple, but I am adamant that it is essential.

Why do we need rest? We know that sleep repairs the body, including the brain—healing cells, processing memories, etc. But we also need a rest that repairs the soul and the mind. A rest that heals our emotions and processes our priorities. Many things drain out of us during the course of every day, and other things build up in us that shouldn't be accumulating there. It is only the process of rest that refuels and repairs, reenergizing us and giving us clarity.

But we're going about it all wrong! First we insist that we can't rest. Too much going on, too much to do. (Subtext: I am very important. The world will fall apart without my constant attention.) We humbly explain that we feel guilty if we sit down for even a moment. (Subtext: I am a martyr. I hope you appreciate all I do.)

Then, when our bodies defy us and force us to slow down, we gravitate to the junk-food version of rest: mind-numbing distractions. You know what I'm talking about. Most of what's on television. Candy Crush. Facebook pages of your friends' friends whom you've never even met. I know all the tricks we use to keep themselves from true rest, because I've tried them all myself.

But I now know: This is not resting. This is crashing. It does not refuel our spirits, give clarity, heal or repair. It is the equivalent of hitting the pause button on our life. Or to use the sleep analogy again, it's like believing that five catnaps every twenty-four hours is enough sleep.

So, what is true rest? I would encourage you to make a study of the Old Testament pattern of Sabbath, as well as the way Jesus challenged the Pharisees' twisted interpretation of it. True rest, quite simply, is to stop working *so that you can listen.* Listen to your life, to your heart, to your loved ones, and most importantly to God. We stop so we can listen, and when we listen, we hear that we can rest.

How does listening happen? In many ways, but I can tell you this: It needs silence and it needs attention. It requires trust—trust to stop working, to let your hands fall idle, to walk away from the constant demands—believing that God is sovereign over your world, sees your needs (and theirs), and can keep you safe without your help. The truth is, we are very uncomfortable with this level of trust, and so we take the time that our bodies are at rest and we crunch it up into noisy distractions so we don't have to think about it.

Be brave. Brave enough to sit in silence. To listen. To contemplate. To sink into Him and know that He is God. To offer up your Dream, your strategies, even your tactics, and listen for a gentle redirection or course correction.

The wonderfully lovely thing about true rest is that unlike short catnaps which cannot take the place of a night's sleep, true rest is very efficient. Brief times of silence and solitude can replace hours of television.

And when you have truly rested, you will have time left for the 20% of the leisure activities that have always given you 80% of your enjoyment. (Did you see what I did there?) The few television shows that you *really* enjoy. Catching up on Facebook with just a handful of friends you want to love well.

So often we chastise ourselves for our time-wasting distractions, telling ourselves to get back to work, be more productive. This week, try the opposite approach. When you are tempted to drift into a mindless distraction because you can't keep pushing forward, take some time instead for true rest. Get outside and take a walk or find a pretty view from inside and spend some time alone, in silence, listening. Being. Loving. Resting.

review

Daily and weekly times of rest are critical, and can be built into our daily routine quite easily, especially if we remove much of the mindless activity that substitutes for it. But there is also great wisdom in taking more extended periods to retreat from your Adventure and get some perspective.

Institute a practice I call the "Weekend Watershed." Remember geography class? A watershed is a point where water divides, on one side running south or west toward one body of water and on the other running north or east toward another. We also use the term *watershed moment* to describe reaching a critical turning point in life. The Weekend Watershed is a weekly practice, occurring sometime between the end of your workday on Friday and the start of it on Monday, in which you take a high-level view of the events of the past week behind you, and a forward look at the plans ahead of you in the coming week. It's a time to review what worked and what didn't, how well you focused, what tactics need changing. Everything you can glean from the past week and put to good use in the future. It's also a chance to collect all the random snippets of life that may have gotten away from you. Notes on your desk, in your purse or wallet, appointment cards you haven't transferred to your calendar. To-do lists in your head. Gather everything that needs to find its way into your Trusted System and get it in there. Then take some time to plan the week ahead. Think through your available time and block out your calendar for times when you'll be working on your Adventure. Make sure there's enough time for everything else. Rearrange, delegate, say no, find focus. You know how to do this by now!

Besides a Weekend Watershed, I recommend a Quarterly Review. This may sound too businesslike for you, but I assure you that it's valuable. Even though I don't advocate creating long-range goals with timelines and deadlines attached to them for the purpose of motivating yourself (it's better to be driven by joy than pressure-filled goals), a ninety-day plan is a useful tool simply for the purposes of direction and saving you time as you choose your next tactics. When you spend some time every quarter curating and lining up the tactics you believe make sense for the next ninety days, you give yourself a leg up on the Weekend Watershed planning you'll do every week.

And now what will probably feel like the most indulgent advice I've yet given: I want you to take a three-day Personal Annual Retreat alone every year. Seriously. I want you to make this happen. You are pursuing an Adventure, living a life of Impactivity. You are currently and in the future doing amazing things to build the kingdom of God. It is worth three days out of your life every year, and worth the inconvenience it may cause, to get alone with God and reorient yourself and your

140

work in the world. Space does not permit me to outline here what I want you to do with these three days, but when you are ready, please read the Personal Annual Retreat Guide available at impactivity.com.

refuel

Speaking of enjoying your life, I want you to take a moment to breathe in what a life of Impactivity can look like, and realize how amazing it's going to be. So many incredible opportunities to offer your skills, gifts, abilities, and passion to the world out of love for God and others. Impactivity is a life of great joy, and there is plenty of room in it for you to enjoy the life and the people and the gifts you've been given.

As part of your times of recharging, spend moments simply savoring all the sensory delights of the world—delicious food and heavenly smells, textures you love, natural beauty and the beauty of the arts. Music and birdsong. I have so many more ideas for you in *Refuel: The Ten Best Ways to Enjoy Your Life*.

Create special times of celebration. Practice gratitude. Learn something new. Take trips. Do something creative. Work on being present and mindful instead of letting your thoughts rush ahead to the next thing. Above all, take extended times to worship and listen to God's voice in your life.

In the process of Impactivity, you have opened space in your heart, your mind, your day, and your home. Enjoy it to the fullest!

journal

_____

_____

_____

_____

_____

_____

_____

_____

_____

_____

_____

_____

_____

_____

14

week five: the recharging

Victoria gave a nod and wink to Julia when she finished with her teaching on the subject of Recharging.

Julia laid her pen across her notes and headed for the kitchen, to retrieve the cheesecake and the apple tart she'd made specially for tonight, at Victoria's request. The older woman had called ahead and asked Julia to keep the desserts in the kitchen until she gave the signal.

The after-hours cafe was silent when she returned except for the overhead music.

Victoria patted the table in front of her, indicating where to place the chilled cheesecake and the still-warm tart. She silently thanked Julia with only a smile, then indicated that she should sit. "We're practicing some silence for a few minutes."

Several minutes later, Victoria spoke again, her voice soft

and low. "Now, raise a hand if you want cheesecake. Apple tart?"

She served each of them in turn with their preference. When they'd all been served, she regained her seat and took an audible deep breath and released it slowly.

Somehow that simple intake of breath caused Julia to do the same, the way a yawn is contagious. But this wasn't a yawn. It was a breath that pulled in peace and exhaled tension.

"Eat slowly, my lovely friends. Enjoy the taste. Enjoy the quiet."

And they did. It was only five minutes, perhaps seven. But it was the most peaceful few minutes Julia had experienced in weeks.

When all the forks had clattered to plates, dishes pushed away from notes and final sips of coffee were taken, Victoria finally spoke.

"How was your dessert?"

Gabrielle sighed. "I think that was the best apple tart I've ever eaten in my life."

"Fantastic, Julia." Melanie wiped her mouth with a napkin. "You outdid yourself."

Julia laughed. "You've all eaten my stuff before. These two were nothing special."

"Is it possible," Victoria asked them all, "that the act of eating in silence, mindful of what you were eating, made the food taste better?"

Her question was met with only thoughtful smiles.

"We rush through so much of life without thinking, without stopping to even enjoy what we are experiencing, so eager to get to the next thing and accomplish the next goal. Is it possible that we rob ourselves of the very life enjoyment we are seeking to create with all our busyness?"

Julia stood and reached to clear the plates, but Victoria stopped her with a touch on her arm. "Leave it, dear. There is time enough later. Relax."

The very sound of that word, *relax,* nearly buckled Julia's knees, and she slid back into her chair with a contented smile.

"So how did you do this week, ladies, with all your Igniting?"

Glances all around, and then Gabrielle spoke up. "I did great! Really great." She bit her lip. "I think."

They all laughed, but Julia could relate. She'd had an extremely productive week, but something seemed off, and she wasn't sure what it was.

"Why the uncertainty, Gabrielle?"

"Well, I made up a plan for the healthy habits I want to incorporate into my life, like you suggested. I decided not to try to start them all at once, but just commit to a few - and I made a chain of them - until I got them to be routine."

"Sounds great so far. Anyone else start new habits this week?"

Each of the other women raised a palm, including Julia. She'd risen early three days this week to go for a brief run, which was quite a feat given how early she had to be at the cafe to start baking, and she'd found time to read her Bible for a bit during the morning lull each day.

Gabrielle continued, "I also made decisions about which of my tactics to focus on first, and scheduled a set time every day to make some progress. I actually made more progress this week than I would have thought possible. Everything seemed to go faster, once I blocked out distractions and really committed to the time. And having all my reminders set up in my system helped to free up my brain, so I wasn't always thinking about what I might be forgetting."

"Wonderful, Gabrielle. We're all proud of you. So, what's the question I hear brewing behind your report?"

"Not a question so much as a... complaint."

Victoria grinned. "Let's hear it. I can take it."

"Well," she paused, wincing as if the words caused her pain to admit, "I'm exhausted."

Wanda grunted in amusement. "You and me both, sister. Our dessert-eating time was so peaceful, I almost face-planted into my apple tart."

Julia hated to admit it, but she was bone-tired, too. Getting up early to run, packing in as much as possible of the bigger picture projects she had designed to build the cafe's customers, creating all her systems and habits and workflows — she didn't think she could keep going at this pace.

Melanie was nodding, too. "I feel really excited about the progress I made this week, and all the plans to do even more, but hearing you talk about Recharging tonight has made me realize that I'm not a machine. I can't work all the time."

"I tried taking a break," Wanda said, "tried sitting with my husband to watch a stupid show on TV. But I felt guilty the whole time."

"Why guilty, Wanda?" Victoria's voice held sympathy.

"Because I know it was a waste of time. I should have been doing something more productive."

Julia leaned forward, arms on the table. "But I think what Victoria is saying is that the "more productive" thing you could have been doing is truly resting, in a way that would refresh you, a way TV never could."

"Exactly!" Victoria lightly slapped her fingers against the table top. "That guilt you feel when you try to relax," and at this she took in all of them with her glance, "is either a false guilt borne out of fear of what others will think if you slow down, or it's a subconscious recognition that you're not actually resting, you're only crashing and killing time."

"Wow." Julia mentally ran through her week and had to admit that she rarely slowed or stopped, partly because she wanted everyone to realize just how crazy-busy she was.

"Ladies, you were not meant to work without ceasing. You must take this teaching to heart, because without it, all your efforts toward Impactivity will be wasted." She paused and let that sink in. "Do you understand this? You can hear the calling of a Dream, get Unshackled to follow it, Design a strategy and Ignite your daily work, but if you do not take time to physically rest, to mentally rest, to review and to plan, to reconnect with God and the people you love, to enjoy your life, and to get re-inspired to pursue your Adventure, then you will fail. You will burn out in a roaring flame of activity that leaves you with nothing more to give. This Recharging is so critical."

Gabrielle touched her empty plate. "It was a good exercise, just to eat in silence and enjoyment. It felt like I'd taken a vacation."

"And yet it was only a few minutes. Do you see how revolutionary this concept can be in your lives? The *efficiency* of silence and solitude and mindfulness is almost beyond understanding."

"I have to admit," Julia said, "there were times this week

147

when I felt like I was really succeeding at everything and yet there was this little question running in the back of my mind, asking 'why am I doing all this if I can't even slow down enough to enjoy it, to enjoy my family or my life?'"

"Exactly!" Gabrielle slapped the table in an exact impression of Victoria and they all laughed.

"Seriously," Gabrielle said, "that was what I was trying to get at earlier when I said I wasn't sure my week was great. It wasn't even the exhaustion—I don't mind hard work or being tired—it was the idea that something important was missing."

Victoria nodded. "You lost sight of your Why. This is natural. We get caught up in the work, head down and plowing through, making great progress. But without a regular lifting of our heads, reorienting, reconnecting, we forget why we're doing any of it."

Julia tapped her lower lip. "It's kind of like we're circling back to Dream when we are Recharging, isn't it?"

"In a way, yes. We need to reconnect with the Dream. But also don't forget, ladies, your life is more than your Dream alone. It is also about loving the people in your life, it's about a deep connection with the God who made you, and an enjoyment of all the good things He gives."

They all seemed to visibly relax into that thought for a moment.

"So I have an assignment for you all." Victoria shrugged apologetically. "Well, several assignments."

"More work?" Julia groaned. She was joking, though. Victoria's assignments were always well worth it.

"Yes, Julia, more work. The hard work of resting! This week I want you to be intentional about trying all sorts of ways to Recharge. Take some notes, ladies." She waited while they got out their notebooks and devices. "I want you to spend some time in solitude and silence. I want you to spend time in prayer, especially bringing all the facets of your Dream to God and listening to what He wants to tell you about it. I want you to set aside focused time to pour love out to at least one member of your family or a close friend. I want you to pick something truly enjoyable to do this week—something celebratory or creative or sensory—and fully experience it without distraction. And this weekend I want you to spend some time reviewing your week and planning for the next one, again bringing your plans to God in surrender. Got it?"

"Will there be time for anything else?"

"Oh, yes. Keep up your habits and make time for your Dream. It will happen."

Melanie closed her notebook. "One more element of Impactivity, right?"

"One more."

Wanda tapped her pen on the table. "I'm not sure I can handle any more than all of this, to be honest."

Victoria smiled. "You wait and see. I think you're going to find this last one surprisingly natural. You've all gotten a big head start, in fact."

Julia went back to clearing the table. "Any clues?"

Victoria shook her head with a mysterious smile. "No clues. But I'll connect with you again next week."

recharge summary

rest

- Understand that the crash that follows your frantic busyness is not true rest
- Take time for silence and solitude, for listening to yourself and to God
- Implement true rest and then invest your free time in enjoyable leisure

retreat

- Set up your Weekend Watershed to review backward and plan ahead
- Commit to a Quarterly Review to sketch out your strategies and tactics for the next ninety days
- Schedule an Annual Retreat to reorient yourself to God's call to Adventure

refuel

- Discover the many ways to slow down and savor the amazing life you've been given

15

connect
find community

For just as each of us has one body with many members,
and these members do not all have the same function,
so in Christ we, though many, form one body,
and each member belongs to all the others.
Romans 12:4-5

E ven before the invention of humans, there was God and
God was somehow Three. In other words, there has
always been, and will always be, this concept of community —
commun*ion*, if you will. We serve a relational God, who
established creation to have relationships even in the animal
world, and certainly among humanity. We need each other. Of
course we do.

But while very few people would make the argument that life is meant to be lived alone or in isolation, I don't believe that many truly understand what this concept of community is all about. At least not the biblical type of community that New Testament life offers. Biblical community involves a level of knowing and being known, of mutual support and transformation, of a sense of mission, that few clusters of Christians ever reach, or even aspire to.

I was first introduced to a vision of deeper community in my mid-twenties, through an unusual and amazing couple who led my "small group" at church. They asked hard questions (even questions without answers!), they loved more deeply and they pursued more actively than anyone I'd yet encountered. I was drawn to them - to their raw honesty and their genuine love. Then they passed out of my life for about a decade. We reconnected in my mid-thirties at a time in my life when I desperately needed community, and this time they introduced me to a whole group of people who were striving and committed to something deeper with each other. Committed to engaging in authentic and vulnerable conversation, to pursuing each others' hearts as well as minds. I was part of this group for only a couple of years until life moved me on, but it was transformational to say the least. I keep in touch with those whose lives changed mine, and am so incredibly grateful for them. In more recent years I have again found a deeper community of people who want to live life alongside me, to know me and let me know them as we walk out our faith together. This Connection is what I want for you.

engage

are we there yet?

There is a good chance you are already part of some type of weekly or monthly gathering of people who share your faith. Perhaps on a Sunday morning or a weekday evening. This group is smaller than an entire church congregation, and likely the place where you share your "prayer requests" and the major highlights and struggles of your life in a summary sort of way. These people know the broad strokes of your life and the big stuff that might be weighing you down and in need of prayer.

It is also likely that the primary function of this group is to study and learn. There has been a tendency in the church over the past several hundred years to imitate academia and to elevate systematic approaches to faith-living, while at the same time de-emphasizing all the other non-teaching gifts and the need for the one-another living we see modeled in the New Testament. The instruction to liberally encourage, to sacrificially love, to bravely rebuke, confront, and point out deception, to lavish each other with honor, to cling to each other like family, to band together in a mission, and to pursue radical unity are often back-burnered as we gather together simply to study and learn. And study and learn some more.

(Should you want to read a few verses about our responsibility toward each other, here is a place to start: Hebrews 10:24, 25; Colossians 3:1; 1 Thessalonians 5:11; Hebrews 3:13; Romans 12:10; Ephesians 4:1-2.)

This kind of community, where masks are dropped and dreams are shared, is transformative because of our deep knowledge of each other and commitment to each other's growth. Without it, we become easy prey to deception. Without people to support us and point us back to our rescue and our freedom, we will become shackled again. One of our strongest defenses against falling into bondage again is to share our specific areas of struggle from the past with people who will be alert to these fears and deceptions creeping back into our life. You will be amazed at how perceptive others can be in pointing out these tendencies when you are blind to them. No doubt you feel you don't (or at least shouldn't) still struggle with these blind spots, but you do.

As you pursue a life of Impactivity, you will face more obstacles than falling back into the need to Unshackle. You will also need help to clarify your often-hazy Dream, need to talk through the vision and strategy of your Design, need accountability around the Igniting of your personal, spiritual, and work habits, and need others to remind you to Recharge. You will need to share both the delightful victories and the crushing discouragements, and need the voices of others to cheer you along your adventure, as you in turn cheer them on.

Are you there yet? Surrounded by people who know you this intimately, who are committed to you this deeply?

If not, read on.

how is community cultivated?

I use the word "cultivated" intentionally. Deep biblical community is not flicked on with the switch of a decision to form it, and it rarely happens naturally. Instead, people (or even just a single person) with the intent and desire to go deeper begin to understand and open up about their desire for this community, then about their definition of it, onward to their

First, seek to break down physical barriers between people. You are family together. Families hug. Families cry on each others' shoulders. Families sometimes even smack each other upside the head.

Break down other barriers, too. Your inborn need to not look foolish must be set aside for true community to develop. The best way to get over yourself and your perfect image is to have fun together. I am talking about more than a "fellowship potluck." I am talking about things like three-legged races and playing charades. Do things together that involve more than talking. Shared experiences that bring you closer. Perhaps it's simply for fun, but these experiences can also be centered around one person's adventure and some help they need in pursuing it.

When you are talking, especially when studying the Bible together, ask tough questions for which you don't have the answer. Avoid clichés. Be comfortable together with unanswered questions, with paradoxes and confusion and struggle. Join each other in that struggle rather than handing out trite, churchy answers that don't really meet people where they truly are and only build walls as those struggling feel they should have it together by now, or at least have it figured out. It's OK to listen and encourage with love, without offering solutions.

When you talk about hard stuff, be willing to say the first thing that comes to mind, without the constant filter to make sure you sound spiritual or smart. Vulnerability and authenticity might be buzz words these days, but they are critical to your community.

Share the times and ways you have been hurt, judged or

criticized in pursuit of your adventure in the past. In sharing the past, you each learn better how to protect each other and support each other in the future.

Be willing to push each other to share your hearts. In fact, *pursue* each others' hearts. Sometimes people want to open up, but are paralyzed from doing so out of fear of being seen as attention-getting or needy. A simple question, like "What's the hardest thing going on in your life right now?" can give a person permission to open up. You will be surprised what will flow from even the quietest and most reticent in your group when given this permission. Simply refuse to let people go week after week as "the quiet one." Everyone desires to share their heart, to be known. To be loved. Some people just need more help than others.

Pray together. And when together, commit to pray only about the specific needs of each other's lives and adventures. You can share other needs and struggles related to friends and family members, but in your prayer times together, focus on the adventures you are each pursuing. It may be the only place in your life where you can openly share your dream and have someone pray specifically over you. In any other group of people you are part of, this might feel strange or self-elevating or embarrassing. Let this group be the place you can safely ask for prayer about your dreams.

Talk together about the importance of habits in the spiritual life and in the adventure. How can you support each other in these habits in between the times when you are all together?

There may be ways in which you naturally fall into intertwining your adventures. If it doesn't happen naturally, be intentional about helping each other with your varied and individual gifts. Take turns focusing on the adventures of each individual person, giving them advice, feedback, and insight, but also practical help outside your official meeting times.

Radically affirm each other. True support happens so rarely in this world that this one aspect of community is almost enough on its own to bind you together in a supernatural way. Sink into this paragraph from author Brennan Manning:

"To affirm a person is to see the good in them that they cannot see in themselves and to repeat it in spite of appearances to the contrary. Please, this is not some Pollyanna optimism that is blind to the reality of evil, but rather like a fine radar system that is tuned in to the true, the good, and the beautiful. When a person is evoked for who she is, not who she is not, the most often result will be the inner healing of her heart through the touch of affirmation."[1]

it isn't always easy

No, it isn't easy. In fact, it's often hard. Hard to show up, hard to be honest, hard to love sacrificially. You will encounter drains on your time and energy that discourage you from your commitment to these people. You will face disagreements or tension within your community that make it easier to avoid than to pursue. You will go through periods of dryness where it seems like nothing is happening, no one is growing, and there is only tedium. Push through. Persevere. Pursue. Find ways to reinvigorate energy, to resolve differences, to challenge each other to shake things up. Take some risks together. Have some fun together. Do something extraordinary.

we want to help

Recognizing that this type of community might not be feasible or even desired among the people you know, we at Impactivity want to help. We've developed some resources for you, including an 8-Week Impactivity Group Study Guide that could be used with your current study group, as well as a guide to Start Your Own Impactivity Group that would meet on an ongoing basis to work together on your Dream. Either of these might be just what you need to find some like-minded people and get started with some shared principles and commitment to Adventure. This study guide may help to give you structure as you get to know each other and grow closer. You'll find other resources in the Connect section of impactivity.com as well.

Or you may find that the online Impactivity Community is a place you can connect with others who will share and support your adventure. We are building a community of amazing people, doing amazing things. You'll find encouragement, wisdom, stories, practical resources and lots of love and laughter there. I sincerely hope you'll join us, whether you have a "real-life" community around you or not. We want to connect with you!

Above all, do not walk out your journey alone. The road is rough and dangerous and often discouraging. The obstacles and shackles are real. The confusion is real. You were not meant to go it alone.

You were meant to Connect.

[1]Brennan Manning, *The Furious Longing of God,* Colorado Springs: David C. Cook, 2009, p. 82-83.

journal

_____

_____

_____

_____

_____

_____

_____

_____

_____

_____

_____

_____

_____

16

one year later

Victoria eased her car into the gravel driveway leading into the woods and pulled behind the single car already parked beside the cabin. It was already dark, with night falling early now that it was November. From inside the cabin a few lamps burned warmly, casting a soft glow into the wooded lot and feeling like a welcome from the long drive.

She lifted her overnight bag from the seat beside her, and was barely out of the car before the front door opened, and a silhouetted figure beckoned from inside.

"Is that her?" Another voice came from inside, and a second figure joined first.

She lifted her hand in a small wave.

"Hey, Victoria! Come in, we're all here."

Melanie hugged her in the doorway, then ushered her into

the beautiful cabin, where Gabrielle, Wanda, and Julia all waited with beaming smiles.

"OK!" Julia clapped her hands together. "Let the First Annual Boss Ladies' Retreat begin!"

Victoria set her bag down and slid her wrap from her shoulders, laughing. "'Boss Ladies'? Is that what you're calling yourselves now?"

Wanda grinned. "You outlawed the Misfit Women name, so we had to come up with a new one."

"Well, I like it." She handed her wrap into Melanie's outstretched hand. "And it's good to see you all."

And it was. It had been several months since the last time she'd dropped into the Java Bean Cafe to check up on the women and see how their steps toward Impactivity were going. She'd given them the sixth element months ago, sharing how important it was that they continued to connect, to support each other and give accountability.

"We're not quite ready for taking our Personal Annual Retreats yet," Melanie had told her over the phone last month. "But we've decided to take a long weekend away together, to do some of the things you've told us about. And we want you there."

She'd been happy to come. At this point, her business was run by trusted managers and her time was hers to spend in whatever ways she found most effective. Over the months, the women had asked her several times just "what she did," but she'd always found creative ways to avoid answering.

Little did they know that *this* was what she did. Meeting with business women, entrepreneurs, and women with a mission to show them a better way than the burnout of over-productivity. There were Java Bean Cafes and Boss Ladies all over the country who were benefitting from Victoria's time.

This weekend, it was just these four, and she would enjoy it.

They gathered in the wood-beamed cozy living room, coffee mugs in hand and a plate of pastries on the table. Victoria recognized the yellow crockery plate from Julia's cafe. In fact, this little cabin was in a way much like the cafe, with a fire burning low in the stone fireplace and the smell of coffee in the air. But it was good to sink into comfortable chairs with her shoes off, settling in for a couple of days with these women who had worked so hard in the past year to pursue the Adventures that God had put in their hearts.

"So," she started, with a smile at them all. "Catch me up."

And so began a glorious review of all the surprises the past year had brought, most notably the way God had woven their journeys together.

"The acting troupe is getting more bookings every month." Melanie was on the edge of her seat, filling them in on the performances of the past few months. "But our favorite venue by far are the women's shelters that Wanda connected us with. It's amazing how a performance can open up the heart of someone who seems so hard, but is in such need. Plus, some of the shelter women are doing some improv performances with us, and I think it really helps them open up about their issues. I wanted to make people in the city more aware of poverty through our performances, but it turns out that our most important presence seems to be with the people in poverty themselves."

"And the women love it," Wanda chimed in. "I hear them

talking about Melanie's group even in the days following their performance, when I'm there teaching classes."

"Tell her more than that, Wanda!"

Wanda grinned. "It's going great. I'm teaching in all three shelters in the city now, a certification program that takes three months to get through. The women find out about it when they first come to the shelter, but even after they've moved on to more permanent housing, they're allowed to come back for the classes. It's great for the new women to see a glimpse of hope."

Victoria loved the way Wanda's energy and positivity had shifted over this past year. She even looked healthier. Probably a result of the habits she'd created to take better care of her physical health and well-being.

Wanda was still smiling and looking at each of them. "But I've been saving some news for this weekend. A call I just got this week."

"Spill it, girl!" Gabrielle rubbed her hands together. "Every time you have news it's so cool."

Wanda took a deep breath. "Someone in Lake City heard about our program and wants me to come there to train them and help set up something similar."

Melanie was taking notes, and added this revelation to the growing list of updates. "That's awesome, Wanda!"

"There's more. My husband and I talked about it, and we're starting to develop a vision for making this a national organization."

There were dropped jaws and wide eyes all around, but Victoria felt no surprise. She had seen this kind of thing again and again with people who started pursuing their dreams in a life of Impactivity.

"Of course, if we do this, we're going to want to step up the timetable on the restaurant changeover."

Julia nodded, smiling. "Oh, that's right—we haven't told Victoria about that part, have we?" She pulled her legs up under her and braced her elbows on her knees. "My husband and I are planning to buy Wanda's restaurant and make it in a second Java Bean Cafe location!"

Well, now that one did surprise Victoria. "That sounds amazing!"

"Yeah, we've gotten so much catering work because of Gabrielle's connections, and with my husband managing the business side of things now, it's really freed me up to train the women Wanda has sent my way. The timing feels right to expand, using the city location to reach even more people."

Victoria turned to the always-smiling Gabrielle. "So, you're making connections?"

"Better than that, actually. I did three weddings this fall, and already have four booked for next summer. And every month I meet with a group of wedding planners, to brainstorm and give each other help. We meet at the Java Bean, of course, and since Julia's team does all the catering for the bridal showers and brunches I arrange, the other wedding planners in my group have been using her, too."

Julia blew a kiss in Gabrielle's direction. "It's been amazing. And we're so excited to open the second location. It's going to have more of an artsy coffeehouse vibe, so Melanie's helping me with that, and we'll definitely have her group perform there often."

Victoria sat back in her chair with a satisfied sigh. "Well, ladies, you have done it. You have truly done it. Besides

165

pursuing your individual Adventures, you have made the beautiful discovery that when each one is following his or her calling, deep community begins to develop around a shared heart."

"Those first few weeks you met with us," Melanie said, "I had no idea how much deeper into all of those six elements of Impactivity we would go."

"Yeah." Wanda's eyes lit up. "I'm really glad you came back a few times and gave us even more to work on." She glanced at the pastry in her hand. "Hey, this is good."

"Very funny." Julia laughed and shook her head, then looked to Victoria. "One of her classes made those for us today."

"Yes, Victoria." Gabrielle reached for one of the recommended pastries herself. "Thanks so much for sticking with us and visiting those few times. It's been hard work, but so worthwhile."

"You are very welcome, my dears. It has been my honor to walk alongside you through the beginning of the journey. And a new year is ahead! I can't wait to hear all the strategies and ideas you are cooking up!"

As the ladies chatted, full of excitement and buzzing with ideas, Victoria only half-listened. Some part of her was remembering back, two decades now, to the time when she had first begun sharing the principles of Impactivity with others. It had started as a simple sharing of the lessons she had learned through her years in business, but as she saw lives begin to change, a Dream had been birthed in her. A new Adventure opening up, to lead others into the discovery and pursuit of their own Adventures. She had Unshackled herself from her business back then, making the sacrifices necessary to do so, and had set about Strategizing how she could offer herself in this way. Once Ignited, twenty years of a slow and steady burn had changed countless lives, and she had enjoyed every day of it.

Here, in this cabin, was a microcosm of her best life's work, her role in the radical kingdom-building God had begun. She had done many things in her lifetime, been more productive than most. But she considered all the leafiness of productivity to be of no value, compared to the fruit she saw before her now.

Her life of Impactivity.

connect summary

engage

- Consider whether your current community is true biblical community
- Seek out others who are like-minded
- Cultivate biblical community by defining it together

pursue

- Break down barriers
- Ask tough questions and avoid clichés
- Share your hurts and your hearts
- Pray over each others' adventures
- Support and affirm each other

where do we go now?

just the beginning

I am thrilled that you have taken this journey with me. If you've read this book straight through in the space of a few hours, then you have only gotten the first taste of Impactivity. You've seen a sketch of what it looked like for Melanie, Julia, Gabrielle, and Wanda, and hopefully what it could look like for you.

I want you to be inspired.

I want you to be excited.

But most of all, I want you to act.

I want you to dream big dreams, and then figure out what's keeping you from pursuing them. I want you to simplify your life and strategize your vision. I want you to get your habits and routines in place, to move everything, including your life-stuff, into a Trusted System. To curate your tasks and projects down to the best of them and then to focus on them for the best part of your day. To end your work and begin your rest at a healthy time each day. To make time to rest and create and enjoy and learn and celebrate and love. Back at the start of this book I gave you permission to read it quickly. Now it is time to give yourself the great gift of reading slowly and taking action.

your hero journey

As you know, I have written many novels, most of them involving some kind of epic quest. I love adventures! There is a concept in fiction, popularized by the mythologist Joseph Campbell, called the "Hero's Journey." The idea is that every hero follows a similar journey, filled with archetypal characters and classic moments. See if anything feels familiar in this storyline: We meet our hero in his Ordinary World, where he is lacking something concrete and usually has an inner need as well. The hero is soon confronted with a Call to Adventure, which he often refuses out of fear. Sometimes a Mentor character comes alongside the hero to convince and help him undertake the Adventure, and sometimes there are terrible circumstances that force him into it. For whatever reason, the hero commits to the quest at hand and experiences the Crossing of the First Threshold into a Special World, where he often encounters hostile Threshold Guardians who try to force him back. Fighting through this first obstacle, he goes on to face many more Tests, to connect with Allies and make Enemies, until the final Climax, featuring the showdown with his biggest Enemy.

Nearly every story you've read and every film you've seen has followed this general pattern. Those that don't follow it are often seen as "experimental." My novels are no exception. The reason we accept and enjoy this repeated pattern is because it resonates with our true experience, the story of our own lives. Perhaps you resist calling yourself the "hero" of your own story. You will want to point to God as that character. But for a moment, walk through that journey I've outlined, seeing yourself as the main character of the life you are living. Just yesterday, you were living in your Ordinary World of mere productivity. Within the pages of this book you have encountered a Call to Adventure, the call to a life of Impactivity. You have many reasons to refuse this Call, and you are no doubt still working through them. It has been my desire to be a Mentor to you, to help equip and guide you into the Special World of Impactivity.

But only you can decide to cross that First Threshold. Only you can decide if you will persevere through the series of Tests that will surely follow and the attacks of enemies who would hold you back. The six elements of Impactivity are not a once-and-done fight. In this series of Tests, you will surely continue to cycle through:

dreaming—to seize a vision of what God can do through you
unshackling—to free yourself from the hindrances that stem from seeking your identity in the wrong places
designing—to sketch the strategy and tactics to support your vision and use a Trusted System to handle the details
igniting—to prioritize your life into the habits, routines and

times of focus to get the work done

recharging—to step away from the work to listen to yourself and to God

connecting—to open yourself to others so you can encourage each other in your journeys

going deeper

We have only scratched the surface of each of these six elements. In our story, Victoria met with the Boss Ladies throughout the year, to go deeper with them into each of the elements. I would love to go deeper with you. At the very least, I would implore you to work your way slowly through this book, stopping to think, journal, plan, and implement steps of action at the end of each chapter.

I have also mentioned the Impactivity website several times through this book, and my hope is that you'll join us there, to avail yourself of the free resources and to find additional help in living out your life of Impactivity. You might also enjoy The Impactivity Podcast, where we get real with all this information and talk about how to live it out every day.

I made reference above to myself as your Mentor on this journey. I hesitate to place myself in that role, because "Mentor" is a big title, for an important person. Most often I want to hide from the perfection and expertise it implies, as well as the responsibility it carries. I have fears, just like you. I worry about what others will think, just like you. I am on this journey, too. But I am learning to step out and be seen, to take risks, to keep growing.

In the last section of our story, Victoria reflects on her

decades of mentoring others toward Impactivity. I am not Victoria as you have seen her in this book, but Victoria is the woman I hope to be when I am older. This book you have read is part of my Adventure. *You* are part of my Adventure. I am blessed to have been part of your journey, and blessed to have you as part of mine.

May we Adventure-on together, undertaking amazing quests for God's kingdom, glorifying Him as we walk out our purpose, always spurring each other on to love and good deeds.

I'll see you on the horizon.

study guide

Please note:
The following study guide questions can be used for individual or group studies.

For a **Leader's Guide to an 8-Week Impactivity Group Study**, please see impactivity.com/group-guide.

before you begin…

1. What do you believe about the idea of *everyone* having a calling on his or her life? What special purpose do you believe you are pursuing?

2. How is busyness keeping you from pursuing a life of lasting impact?

3. How is a lack of clarity keeping you from this "impactivity" life?

4. How has guilt or embarrassment over a dream kept you stuck?

5. Read Ephesians 2:8-10. What do you believe the "good works" in verse 10 refers to? Are they general for everyone, or do you believe that God has given you certain gifts, skills and abilities to do in this Kingdom He's building?

6. Read 1 Timothy 6:6-8 and Proverbs 13:4. When you look at your life, how satisfied do you feel with where you are, and with your goals for your life? How do you determine what is contentment and what is complacency or a resistance to growth?

questions for chapters 1 – 4:

1. How much do you identify with the person described in the first few pages? How important is productivity to you?

2. What did you think of Tracy's story of hitting bottom because of her drive to do more and to succeed? Have you experienced anything similar? If so, how did you handle it?

3. Do you agree that your life should be one of thriving joy, rather than exhaustion and chaos? How does the suffering mentioned in John 16:33 and the self-denial in Luke 9:23 fit with the picture of the abundant life of John 10:10?

4. Do you identify with any of the four women who meet at the Java Bean Café?

   - Melanie, with the part-time office job who is trying to hold onto a dream she's had since college
   - Julia, working hard in her own business but not sure it's worth it
   - Wanda, exhausted from years of driving hard to make her business into a success
   - Gabrielle, at the beginning of an exciting career but unsure how to proceed

5. What did you think about the concept of work/rest balance instead of work/life balance? Do you feel like work is the opposite of life?

6. If you use the metaphor of a highway to describe your life, are you more likely to be in the passing lane and veering onto the left shoulder to pass others, or are you usually in the right lane, even pulling off onto the shoulder and idling?

questions for chapters 5 – 6:

1. What kinds of feelings did this chapter on Dreaming stir inside you?

2. Did you make the three lists as Tracy encouraged you to? What did you find at the intersection of your three lists – the place where your skills and gifts intersect with your passion and can be offered to a world in need?

3. How is it possible to pursue a Dream for your life without becoming self-centered, or making your life all about yourself?

4. In what ways are you already pursuing this Dream? Did this chapter make you want to change anything? If you're not pursuing it, what do you think has been stopping you?

5. Read Genesis 2:15. Do you believe that work is part of the curse? Even if you don't believe it, do you sometimes act like it's a "necessary evil"?

6. Do you agree that all work is sacred? Have you ever felt that the work you do, or the Dream you have, is less important than others' dreams?

7. What did you think of how Victoria was able to connect Gabrielle's desire to build a wedding-planner business to the deeper reasons it was so important to her? Can you find that deeper Why in your dream?

questions for chapters 7 – 8:

1. If you are wanting to pursue a Dream, how can you create the time and space in your life?

2. How has the spiritual component to the clutter, big purchases, and over-busy schedules we are often shackled with kept you from pursuing a Dream that you believe God has given?

   ■ If you are shackled to Other People's Adventures, saying yes too often to what people need, how can you get free?
   ■ How will you make a change in your cluttered home or expensive possessions so you can think clearly or find the time and clarity to pursue dreams?
   ■ Will you make a change to your budget to free up time?
   ■ How does your hectic schedule and high level of productivity sometimes fool you into thinking you have Impactivity or are pursuing your Dream?

3. Read Galatians 5:13. How do we sometimes turn even our serving into a type of bondage? If you sometimes feel in bondage to the commitments you've made to serve others, how is this bondage different than the loving service this verse is talking about?

4. If you believe that freedom is possible, how will you get there?

5. Victoria speaks some very challenging words, especially to Melanie, about making hard changes in her life. How were you challenged yourself by Victoria's words?

questions for chapters 9 – 10:

1. Read Psalm 90:17. Do you regularly ask God to establish the work of your hands? If you are trying to create something (a business, an organization or ministry, a creative product), how is it biblical to ask God to give it success?

2. Are you by nature a goal-setter? What did you think of Tracy's advice to avoid using goals to define your Dream?

3. Are you able at this point to articulate your Dream, your Vision? If so, what is it?

4. What are some of the Strategies you have in mind to accomplish your Vision?

5. Does the idea of brainstorming lots of Tactics sound exciting or overwhelming? Why?

6. Do you use your email Inbox as a catch-all for things that need to be filed, to be done, and all kinds of other things? How many emails would you guess are in your Inbox right now? How would it make you feel to see an empty Inbox every day?

7. Do you have a Trusted System to keep track of everything in your life? Do you wish you had one?

8. Is all of this "designing" part of your relationship with God, or separate from it?

questions for chapters 11 – 12:

1. How were you challenged by the intentional way Tracy explains implementing habits, with a system of triggers, behaviors and rewards set up to remove the necessity of choosing what to do next?

2. What kinds of good habits would you like to incorporate into your life?

3. If you find it difficult to prioritize, always tending to see everything, or nothing, as a priority, how can you make changes?

4. Read Proverbs 14:23. Is your tendency to sometimes be "mere talk" rather than "profitable toil"? If so, in what ways have you seen this behavior lead to "poverty"?

5. If you were to divide your tasks and projects into two categories: your Adventure and everything else, and then simplify the ideas for your Dream down to the best 20%, does it suddenly become simpler to know what to do next?

6. How challenging is it for you to focus your decisions on one project at a time? How about focusing your attention on a single task at a time? How could you improve?

7. How much time might you gain by outsourcing, delegating, and cutting out wasted time? What are the challenges involved in this kind of thinking?

8. In what ways do you identify with Melanie, finally getting time to work on your Dream but then not knowing what to do first and getting distracted by the rest of life?

questions for chapters 13 – 14:

1. What does Tracy's admonishment to truly rest do to your spirit? Do you fear silence or do you crave it?

2. Tracy speaks of the need for trust, if we are to truly rest. "The truth is, we are very uncomfortable with this level of trust, and so we take the time that our bodies are at rest and we crunch it up into noisy distractions so we don't have to think about it." How has this been true for you?

3. In what ways do you think the practice of the Weekend Watershed, the Quarterly Review and the Annual Retreat would be helpful for you? Do you think they are possible for you?

4. In the previous chapters we read Proverbs 14:23, which said that there was profit in toil. Now Psalm 127:1-2 says that our toil is in vain. How do we reconcile these two ideas?

5. How do you regularly take time to really enjoy your life? To slow down and experience all the wonderful things and people you've been given? How can you do better, and what do you think it would do for your life and your Dream?

6. What are your thoughts about the concept of Sabbath rest?

7. The ladies in the Java Bean Café experienced just a few minutes of silence and sensory enjoyment, and then were given some homework by Victoria. Can you try your own "refueling" exercise this week, and perhaps take on the homework she gave them?

questions for chapters 15 – 16:

1. Have you been part of a true biblical community like Tracy describes? If not, is there a longing for it in your heart?

2. How difficult is it for you to be open with others, to share both struggles and dreams? Sometimes the sharing of dreams is even more difficult. Our admitting of our flaws makes us seem humble, but to be open about our dreams may sound arrogant. Do you agree? Where is the place that you can fully express both?

3. Read Romans 12:4-5. How does the forming of one body complement the idea of individual dreams each person is uniquely gifted and skilled to pursue?

4. How can you move toward true community and find a place where you can support and be supported in this way? What actions can you take immediately? What values would you put in place?

5. How did you feel about the end of the Java Bean Café ladies' story? Did it inspire you to seek out community of your own?

wrapping up:

If you've thoughtfully read through this book and worked through these study guide questions, you've undertaken a very important journey.

But in many ways, your journey is just beginning, because it's the journey of your life. Don't be discouraged if you still feel a bit unsure about your Dream, or are still fighting to bring it to life. It's a process!

No book, no matter how thought-provoking, can accomplish what time, intention, and commitment will bring you. So keep working at it.

As you finish this "first round" of pursuing Impactivity, we encourage you to do two things as soon as possible:

1. Get your thoughts recorded somewhere – on paper, digitally, even in a voice recording – so you can revisit what you've learned as you go forward.

2. Find others to support and encourage you, either in your local community, online, or within the Impactivity Community. Come share your story with us.

Your life is an Adventure!

about the author

 Bestselling author and successful entrepreneur, Tracy has been where you are. A super-busy novelist, retail business owner, college professor, and mom of four, she knows what it's like to set the world on fire but get burned out in the process. After years of feeling different than most of the women she knew, her desire is to walk alongside other like-minded Christian women who want to make a lasting impact with their lives both within and outside the four walls of their homes.

**Connect with Tracy
and the rest of the Impactivity Team**
www.impactivity.com
facebook.com/impactivity
twitter: @impactivity2day
instagram: @impactivity

spinning your wheels?

You're longing for life to be an *adventure*, but instead it seems like you're *stuck*…

Underneath the image of success, you are questioning whether you are busy about the right things or perhaps focusing on the unimportant.

You have a nagging fear that you're wasting time or not getting enough done. The busyness is starting to get to you, to weigh you down with exhaustion.

In *Dream: Discover the Adventure of Your Life* you are invited to a journey of self-discovery.

Dive deeper into the Dream element and get even more help:

- » How to identify your true calling in life, a dream unique to your heart
- » How to create a daring life of adventure that is custom designed for you
- » How to find clarity and know where to focus your time and energy
- » How to break through fear, guilt and distraction to pursue your calling with passion, risk and joy
- » How to pursue what you love to create a business, organization or cause

It's time to *listen to yourself* and to your *unique calling*, discover the dream that lies buried within, and find the *courage* to bring it to life!

This workbook is jam-packed with practical wisdom, exercises to walk you through a process of discovering your Dream, and hands-on advice for how to pursue the Adventure you were made for.

Get *Dream: Discover the Adventure of Your Life*
impactivity.com/dream-workbook

looking for your next study topic?

Something *energizing* and *different* that may even draw *newcomers* to your group?

The Impactivity 8-Week Study Guide for Groups is your Leader's Guide for taking a group of women through the book Impactivity: How to Shift Your Productivity into Lasting Impact.

In this Group Study, you'll walk through eight weeks of…

» diving deep into the dreams each of you has for your life and how to uncover the calling of God in those dreams
» getting free to pursue that calling
» designing a plan for following through
» getting organized about the work
» learning how to stop working to embrace true rest
» becoming a supportive community that will go on encouraging each other long after the study is over

Purchase a single copy of the *Leader's Guide*, and make sure each woman has a print or digital version of the book Impactivity when you begin your life-changing journey together.

Get *Impactivity Study Guide for Groups*
impactivity.com/group-guide